This book was published in Scotland March 2018
by Completely Novel

Author Rev Judith Wills M.Div PCH

Edited by Mary Jo Aloi CCH

Cover design by Gillian Mason

ISBN 978-1-7872 32-24-2

www.themystichealer.co.uk

Dedications

This book is dedicated to all my teachers, colleagues, clients and students as each and every one taught me so much. Thank you for that opportunity for growth.

Thanks to my friends and family for all the gifts of love, inspiration and challenge they offered.

I would like to thank Mary Jo, dear friend, colleague and editor from heaven for her vast wealth of experience, wisdom and patience; without whom this book would not have happened.

The Mystic-Healer
Presence: The How of Healing....

Modern Science has come to
understand that matter is only
condensed energy......Sooner or later
science will also discover that what it
calls `energy` is only condensed
psychic force – which discovery will
lead in the end to the establishment of
the fact that all psychic force is the `
condensation` purely and simply of
consciousness, i.e. spirit."

Valentin Tomburg
20th century philosopher

Contents

Introduction

I have been practicing as a Classical Homoeopath for nearly thirty years and an Interspiritual Minister for the last sixteen years. In that time, I have expanded and refined my understanding of health and healing in light of the spiritual journey and come to realize the dynamic role the practitioner plays in the healing journey. The practitioner can only `take` the other to the extent of the practitioners awareness. This limitation could include the practitioner's inability to see the interconnectivity of all symptoms, physical, mental, spiritual and emotional, as well as an understanding of living in Divine alignment upheld in spiritual qualities. Unencumbered by limitation, the Mystic-Healer is the vehicle for soul healing, for mystic–healing.

The world view each person perceives is their "take" on this world and determines the criteria they apply to each decision they make and, consequently, their experience of the results of their own choices. We do indeed create our own reality.

In my experience, all pain, whether mental, emotional or physical, comes from our separation with the Source of All, God, however you refer to the Divine. The more we explore, delve, experience and surrender to this void of separation and the impact it has on life in all ways, the more the gap between the spiritual world and health and healing closes.

This book takes us on the journey from sickness through healing to a place of health and unity. The book describes the role the Mystic-Healer has in extending the personal journey to others in a mutually healing relationship.

It opens up a pathway to reconnect with the healing world in a powerful transformative trans-therapeutic model, a modern approach to spirituality, unencumbered by religion.

For the purposes of this book God, Divine One, Higher Presence all refer to the same 'presence', please use your personal term in these places.

This book is not a theological treatise or scholarly tome, it is, however, a synthesis of the practice of spirituality, the philosophy of health and the art of healing. It is written through the lens of my experience which is a Christian and homoeopathic background so please look beyond that language to the greater commonalities inherent in what is being discussed.

This book bridges the world of health and healing with the spiritual journey and shows how we, as practitioners, can be a healing catalyst for ourselves and others. It aims to highlight how our beliefs become our biology and how healing must originate at its source to be transformational.

This book is intended for anyone working in the health and healing disciplines. It is intended to give an overarching understanding of why health, healing and the spiritual journey are irrevocably intertwined. It is fully appreciated that each section, and subsection could be a book in its own right and is worthy of being studied at length; however for the purposes of this book the sections and subsections are just introductions to each topic.

Further, this book is intended as a companion to the experiential exploration of these concepts in the online course, "The Way of the Mystic-Healer."

Health - *The Goal*

It seems a strange thing to define health in a book which is aimed at the health care professional who, presumably, already is working from a definition of health. The aim is to revolutionize this view and to bring to conscious awareness and clarity to what is really meant when we use the word. To those working with a wholistic totality, health is discovering and moving toward alignment with the core mission of the person. Samuel Hahnemann wrote in the seventeenth century *"The physician's high and **only** mission is to restore the sick to health, to cure, as it is termed."* For the Mystic-Healer, health is to reunite with her God, her sense of and relationship with the Divine.

Often denied or overlooked, the spiritual component of health, gives existence meaning and context, without which life is like soup in a basket and health has no meaning.

In health, one opens to his soul, to feel the inter-connectedness of All and know his part is vital within It and as It.

A clearly defined understanding of what `health and healing` mean to each practitioner ensures focus which then becomes an invaluable assessment tool. The practitioner's definition of health has its own inherent criteria for evaluation of not only her own personal journey but also the progress of the patients with whom he works. To discover your definition, the criteria you may unconsciously apply when working with people, you need to discern your understanding of your Divine Mission or Purpose.

Divine Mission /Purpose
You can discern your Divine mission by diving within and re-
discovering your passion, reconnecting with your raison d'etre.
When you are fulfilling your core passion, you come alive. This
passion can be the driving force behind living a fulfilled life.

When we do this, we offer the Divine a channel to flow through
us. As God is able to act in the world through us in our mission,
we are suffused with energy, passion replenishing itself,
creativity flowing. Living our calling, pursuing our Divine
mission is a healing catalyst.

With this sense of purpose, comes focus, awareness, willingness
to extend to others and reach out freely from the wholeness that
comes with living `in passion`. Einstein once said "Find your
passion, make it your profession and you will never work
again." We could add `and be much healthier too`!

When we can't `live` our calling, we can adjust our focus to the
quality of how we work. So we may sit taking dictation or
working in a call centre each day, but if our focus is on the
quality of all we do, then it immediately transforms what we do
into sacred action.

Union / Re-union
All of the main traditional religions assure us that the goal of
life is to be at One with God, to love our brother *AS* our self.
Does this offer us insight into the ultimate definition of health?
Is health, in fact, union with the Divine? And if so, maybe
healing is the portal through which we return home to God, the
true meaning of re-union.

Lao Tzu said "The movement of the Tao consists in
`returning`". Is `returning` the very dynamism that moves us
closer to Oneness with the Divine and being `home`? If God is
home, then returning could be considered the healing journey, it
is the vehicle taking us into greater awareness of the Divine,
opening hearts to the experience of this relationship.

The great Sufi poet Hafiz tells us that the journey to God will happen, and asks, "do you want to get there by stretcher or by dancing?" The choice is ours.

Authenticity

Pursuit of this `potentised` awareness of health will require exploration of the qualities or truths that define it and a willingness to embrace and embody each quality. One of the first steps to take when deciding to go `home`, is to fully own who we are, to be authentic. `To thine own self be true`.

The willingness to go within is already demonstrating how we have stepped out of who we were previously. Our authenticity will be as deep as our honest willingness to accept all we find when looking within.

Thomas Merton, a Cistercian monk from the 20th century spoke of his definition of being a saint, and said that "The problem of sanctity and salvation is in fact the problem of finding out who I am and discovering my true self". He was clear on the power of authenticity and going in deep enough to find the Divine within.

Authenticity becomes a dynamic openness and relationship with the Divine flow; inauthenticity, from the lies we tell ourselves or others, creates boulders which restricts the smooth flow of Divinity to infuse us. To be fully human is to be fully Divine, our true self is one with God.

The places where we step out of authentic alignment are areas in need of exploring, of loving and accepting, of forgiveness both for ourselves and for others.

Go beyond the fears of being authentic! Dive in. Explore. Open to your true self and go beyond the judgment. See yourself, naked and open, see how you glow in that courageous vulnerability. From here there is nothing to fear, nothing to be taken away, nothing that can be used to hurt you. In this authenticity you meet God, God in self, God in other. Here you step into freedom, here you are truly liberated.

What a gift, to move toward loving yourself in every expression of your `you-ness`. You are the most amazing you possible. How wonderful to surrender within! What a relief to not need to pretend anymore, to not smile on the outside whilst gritting your teeth within, to not look for or need approval from anyone, to not do things you really don't want to do, to release the need to be someone else. There is no need to emulate another, to hero worship, to envy or long to be anyone other than the perfect person you are. How wise to know you are perfect exactly as you are, much like the lily of the Bible, it seeks neither to spin nor toil. It is just perfect in its `lily-ness`. Who are we to say we are not perfect? This is heresy, in effect saying that we know better than God. All this playing small is as much arrogance as playing big.

When we are fully ourselves, we open the portal to the Divine, the more fully we embrace the truth within, the greater the link. Authenticity provides a magnifying glass for the soul. When we open up to the truth within, we can see all the areas in need of healing. Temper the inner exploration with compassion and gentleness. When it is a challenge, the prayer to God might simply be "Beloved, Help me be willing to see. Amen."

Authenticity is a magnet, if we can suspend the tendency for judgment, we will draw people to us who want to live up to the honesty in *our* being-ness. Our authenticity refines our energetic field. In our work life, our authenticity will allow our patients and clients to share more deeply as our authenticity dictates our non-judgmentalism. Owning and releasing all that we have ever done, every thought, word or action that has not been from our highest place offers others security in revelation, they will naturally want to meet us as deeply as they can.

Ultimate homoeopathy is `action through in-action`

Jesus was authentic when he overturned the money changers tables in the synagogue. He was true to his beliefs. He did not hold onto it. Authenticity means being fully who we are NOW, this very moment in time. The energy it takes to hold onto and project an image of how we would like to be perceived is a black hole for vitalism. It can suck the life out of us with illness, the only possible result as our souls desperately try to reconnect.

Authenticity is an exposing of your true self and this is the part we spend most of our lives avoiding. Where are you fully exposed and where do you hide? Start with the physical level, then the mental and emotional levels. How do you present in public, at work and with friends? The dichotomy within your being is the source of all illness, which also means it is the route to healing. The more fully you inhabit your own body (heart, mind and soul) the more at peace you will be. Honesty is a powerful healing dynamic re-empowering us with all we need to heal.

The more honest we are, the deeper the place at which we connect with others. Herein lies the seeds of true intimacy. The self-honesty of the Mystic –Practitioner determines the depth to which the other can share. The Mystic-Practitioner's energetic state *is* their authenticity. If the patient's self-honesty exceeds the Mystic-Practitioner's self-honesty, the patient risks judgment and rejection.

In health terms this honesty is phenomenal. You can review yourself as your own laboratory, being constantly aware of how you are responding in each and any given moment to shine the light of self illumination within. A response to any situation creates a feeling, albeit experienced *only* briefly, felt before being either embraced or judged inappropriate. If this is suppressed the ball of energy released in response to the situation has been stashed into the cells of the body somewhere. The healing dynamic has to employ energy to keep the emotion suppressed. When this starts to move to the physical level, it can emerge in ailments and injuries, in addictions of all kinds.

This then multiplies the original inner `lie`, exponentially setting the scene for many other illness and diseases to manifest. The worst outcome of this process is that it stops our journey into self awareness, the path home to Oneness in the unity of all. By our denial we stay, stuck like Atlas, ever destined to push the lie up the hill and suffer as it rolls to the bottom. Why? Because we chose to believe another human being, yes, we let another flawed human being convince us that we have to be someone we are not to be acceptable. Let's raise a glass to grumpy old men and women who don't care what you think!!!

Integrity
Integrity is the sister of authenticity, having discovered the real you, the next step is living in truth. Integrity is when you align your core beliefs, whatever they may be, with your thoughts, words and actions. This is living congruence in three dimensions. It is moving from the edges of a tornado where we are being battered by the flying detritus of our life, to the eye of the storm where all is still and calm.

Illness often originates from times we have stepped out of integrity. When fear has such power over us that we are prepared to `lie` to palliate it, our energy flow is altered.

We move from the winding meandering deep river of life to the forced cemented channels of limited size. Here we risk losing our dynamic connection with all of nature, where we are One. We have stepped into the energy field of the human condition, where we are limited by fear, surrounded by distrust and consequently growing the mould of perfidy!

When we are willing to be fully who we are, self aware, and living in integrity, our inner `knowingness` is transformed into a deeper gnosis, a heartfelt experiential knowledge encompassing intuition and the collective unconscious.

At first stepping out of alignment may be slight and subtle, perhaps a gentle erosion of congruence, maybe a desire for peace, or to please another, or a lack of confidence in the face of stronger views on a subject. This erosion is repeated over the years, daily, weekly, monthly. We give a little and then give a little more until, after many years, this accumulation catches up and is ready to re-calibrate the outer world in order to reflect the mutated inner world we have created. Becoming first aware of, and then willing to rediscover the truth of who we really are is the journey towards healing.

Beliefs
Beliefs underpin your worldview, the way you see the external world and your own place in it.
If the belief is "the world is a scary place", then there will be fear. This tends to result in looking to palliate the inner fear by insuring, locking, protecting and controlling in any way. As we believe, so we perceive, as we perceive so we behave.
Identifying the unconscious beliefs you hold is a step toward freedom, when you can identify them, you can release them.

What we believe in determines our lifestyles. If our belief is in anything less than love, then `death` is the only result. It may be a series of little deaths in daily disappointments, daily failures and sense of inadequacy that cannot be stilled, but it is still daily death to hope.
Belief is what drives us, gets us out of bed in the morning, what animates us.

If our belief is in love, another name for Higher Power, Source of All, then we have hope with us at all times to escort us through life.This belief provides a deep contentment coming from a positive self image. It has been recorded many times over that people with positive loving faith live longer and happier lives than those without. There have been many surveys supporting this including a recent survey by The Gallup-Healthways Well-Being Index who asked a random sample of Americans across the country to rate or describe how healthy they were in several categories, such as overall quality of life, emotional health, physical health, healthy behavior habits, job satisfaction and access to doctors and other health resources, all of which came back higher for people with a spiritual belief.

Belief that determines decision making. Belief feeds life. Some beliefs nourish, others starve. Belief is behind greater self-esteem, more acceptance of others and a deeper sense of friendship, and community.

Focusing on a spiritual or inner self awareness encourages an understanding of values and tools that support the deepening of this journey. It encourages self-responsibility and a mature emotional outlook in discerning one's place in the world. Belief can offer a safe forum to explore the issues that arise through life. Belief offers a goal, and a structure to support the journey like a spiritual zimmer frame.

The discrepancy between what one thinks is one's belief and the truth of the *belief that one acts* on creates illness.

This is the gulf between core mission and the reality of life. It is the incongruence that disturbs us, that has us perpetually in two minds. The Muslims call this the Jihad, the inner war of the two voices. One represents the insatiable desires of the ego, insatiable in that it has needs it wants met, and once met will soon be sated again and want more; the other is the voice for Love, where we surrender to Divine Will and think of others as well as ourselves.

Our life, our jobs and friends have emerged from whichever voice we listen to. We will meet and befriend people who match us on the journey; our beliefs are met in their beliefs. Or perhaps more accurately, our disconnection from our belief is matched in their disconnection, that our chosen method of distraction is also their chosen method of distraction?

If a river represents the flow of our Divine mission, then a canal may be our reality. Another way to view this disconnection is as the delusion. If, as purported so far, the only life is within the greater context of God, Source of All; then the only truth is that of a life lived in complete alignment with the Divine. Anything less is believing a false truth, an illusion; living a lie. To live life based on a lie is building on shifting sands.

When our belief is refined and clear and we live in congruence with it, we experience living authentically and with integrity.

A life of incongruence is unstable and will erode leaving an instability that has to be perpetually altered and adjusted to keep afloat. This will likely result in aimlessness, an unanchored bobbing around at the whim and will of life. Living authentically with integrity is the internal anchor for security and trust offering a solid framework in which to live life to the fullest. This leads us towards living with internal validation. No matter what our belief is, it is our ability to live 'to' it, to live in alignment and in integrity, that determines our health. Our role as Mystic-Healers is to walk in our deepest alignment and travel with others who choose health and healing.

Inner validation
One of the greatest gifts of knowing our deepest beliefs is the peace that comes when we are able to inner validate through our beliefs. Inner validation is the result of a belief in something higher than oneself, some Divine energy that is greater than humanity and able to surround, infuse, anchor and secure.

External validation leaves the individual dependent on those around them for reinforcement that they are OK, that they matter. However, as every human being is challenged with finding their own deep still voice within, why do we so willingly believe another rather than trust our Self? When we rely on other people's approbation of us, we are left in a state beyond exposed; we are left open to abuse of the grossest nature. If we do this, we have deferred our faith in ourselves to another whose opinion may depend on their mood in any given moment.

Inner validation is part of the triad indicating healthy self-regard, along with self-respect and self-awareness. Inner validation is a vital component in the journey toward health. Carl Rodgers referred to it as unconditional self-regard. Believing in the veracity of the God within is stepping closer to living in peace.

There is, of course, a wee challenge with self-validation and that is to be clear that the voice heard and responded to is indeed the voice of God and not the ego chattering loudly. The Course in Miracles offers guidance in this matter. It says there is only one continuum in life, one end is one hundred percent Love, God, Unity, and the other end is one hundred percent fear, ego, specialness, separation. The Course in Miracles is a modern textbook offering a way to release attachments. It has a lesson a day for a year with the aim of releasing all attachments to everything allowing us to start deconstructing our perceptions which are then transformed through the lens of forgiveness to a non-attached, loving and forgiving worldview. For genuine discernment to take place, each thought and decision must be evaluated by its potential outcome. Will this thought or deed take us closer to love and unity with others, is it expansive and unifying or does it contract us in fear, keep us separated from others or thinking we are special? One is the Voice for God, the other the voice for the ego.

Self-validation is essential in freedom as it allows us to swim against the tide and have a deep `gnosis` of who we are which supports us living in the world. The tide in society is going in the opposite direction to the spiritual journey which makes the pursuit of the true spiritual goal, wholistic health, all the more challenging. True liberation is living authentically with the freedom to trust yourself, opening life up to be fully lived and experienced.

Liberation
Health is the result of liberation, a release from the mind games the ego plays with us. Part of our desire to come home, the yearning spoken of earlier, is the knowledge that only through

liberation from the chains with which the ego binds us can we experience the freedom that true health offers. But these egoic ties may bind us tightly, trussing our minds in barbed wire chains that keep us tightly bound in delusion. Liberation is seeing the truth exactly as it is. It is stepping out of believing the stories we have woven around our lives, the narrative we create to justify our behaviour. As mentioned earlier, `as we believe, so we behave`, our lives are testament to our conscious and unconscious beliefs.

Does it not behoove us to look within, to be fully conscious and explore the inner world? We cannot be liberated without awareness. Goldfish born in a small bowl will still, if transferred to a large bowl, swim within the previous bowls parameters. Elephants tethered by light chains when young stop testing the chain and when they are fully grown are held in place by a chain they could snap with their trunks. How much of this do we do to ourselves?

From infancy to adulthood we test and push, stretch the boundaries of our world until we have what we think we want, then we stop pushing. Might it be wise to commit to re-exploring on a regular basis the boundaries we set ourselves? Perhaps we have moved beyond the structures given in childhood.

How much do we restrict ourselves as we live lives directed by others to palliate *their* inner fears? Liberation is the verb in freedom, it is what we are offering all the people who come to us for help in whatever way; it might be liberation from a physical pain, a mental block, emotional distress or a spiritual void. Whatever they come with, this is what we seek for them, this is where we join with them to companion them through the portal that the pain, block, distress or void offers to freedom beyond.

Universal truths
`The Universal Truths` or `Perennial Philosophy` form the common ground of the different religions. From the earliest of

time to the present day, the same core observations and understandings appear. These have been lost to many people for centuries by the pervasive need of humanity to be right. If I need to be right, then you must be wrong, so it is easy to see how many religions have lost the core message in an attempt to control, to subjugate and to chase power and wealth. Diving in deeply, we find the place where the core messages of the religions merge and share truths.

Gather together any group of people living deeply in their faith, and their conversation will be peppered with `oh's` and `ah's` of recognition as they realise that the core place of all their traditions is one, and the only differences are semantic. Words, phrases and focus may differ, yet all encompass the diamond of spirituality. Each tradition highlights a different facet of Divinity, Christians focus on forgiveness and loving your brother as yourself, Buddhists concentrate on compassion, with Islam highlighting surrender. Sufis polish their hearts with devotion and The Earth Traditions revere the natural world. Combine these facets and what a rich and inspiring jewel the diamond of Divinity is.

All acknowledge that the body is the vehicle for the spirit and the spirit is the anima/animus of the body, together they create a union. Here on earth, the body and soul become one. All acknowledge that the world we perceive is a result of delusion, separation and duality. That what is commonly thought to be held as true and real is nothing of the sort, it represents the point at which humanity moved into duality as it separated from union with God and each person began to view the world through the lens of their own relationship with the world and their place in it.

The religious and philosophical traditions offer different structures to support the journey out of delusion back to unity, be this Ten Commandments, the Sermon on the Mount, or the Eightfold Noble Path. The goal is enlightenment and rebirth into Oneness with the Divine. Releasing the ego dissolves the suffering of living in duality, liberating us from delusion. It increases our ability to extend love, compassion, devotion, reverence and all the gifts of spirit to others.

What is in one is in the whole, proven last century by the holograph where it was explicit that each part was the whole in miniature. How far down can we fragment this? Is this an image of the Divine within that we can grasp? Is this not a poetic image, to realise that no matter how much mankind can break down into ever-minute particles the building blocks of humanity, running throughout the hologram is the Divine.

God dwells in the place with no fear, the merging with another. How many of us can truly identify with this profound idea, that we are part of God's hologram?

When we focus on the indwelling Divine, we are in heaven. When we focus on where the ego kicks and screams in its efforts to keep us separate, special, unique, we are in hell. Crazy as it sounds, that is where most of us focus, on our failings, perceived through judgements based on egoic ideas promoting separation. The ego is very clever as it seduces us with the notion of inclusion by promoting separation! We see this play out in so many ways, like body image or education.

If you lose enough weight you will be loved... ergo you are not loved now, drawing your attention away from the Divine and onto the latest diet fad. Or maybe you should sit for that exam so people value you, same process again, the ego telling you that you are not worthy as you are and need to be someone else to be `seen`. The Universal Truth is of our divine and blessed Oneness with each other and God.

Gnosis
Gnosis is Divine knowledge, it comes from our hearts where the Divine lives viscerally within. Caroline Myss offers, "the three categories of knowledge are information, active knowledge and gnosis, knowledge revealed through Grace."

Gnosis is knowledge of the experience of the Divine. It is where we have awakened to the truth of who we are, left the deluded ego behind and are willing to see with clear vision the reality, the inner truth. Many times it has been written, `the truth shall set you free`. Identifying truth is gnosis, the ability to discern between the voice of ego and the voice of the Holy Spirit, is gnosis.

In homoeopathic terms this is the MM of the centesimal range, the similimum in self-awareness, it is the bull's eye of living on earth. It is the ultimate inner witness, quietly, gently watching our thoughts staying always in alignment. It neither judges nor scolds us, it just honours its place. When we connect with it, the experience is visceral. Gnosis is a depth of understanding that nothing else comes close to. There is no question, no doubt about it, we just `know`. When all is in alignment, when all thoughts come from love, that is gnosis.

Alignment with spirit
These are the gifts that bless us when we live as Mystic-Healers which, in turn, we extend to everyone we encounter in any capacity. It is here that we see the results of the healing relationship when patients and others begin to realize and experience these blessings.
Blessings of alignment with the spirit include qualities such as agape, joy, peace, patience, kindness, faithfulness, gentleness, humility, contentment, and simple presence.

The gifts that come from living to your highest include Agape, Greek for Love, Caritas in Latin and Cariad in Welsh! Agape, is the purest of love, the love that asks for nothing in return, it is seeking the best for the other at all times; it is humble and genuine in this love. It is the truly unconditional love that we all wish to receive and extend. Agape is much deeper love than erotic love, filial love, and paternal love, because it doesn't form attachments. Parental love is the closest many people get to experience the giving and receiving of such depth of pure love. Agape, pure love, always sees the other's inner perfect self. It is from Agape that forgiveness comes, a deep true heartfelt release of resentment and grudges.

Joy is also a result of our choosing to align with Divine will.

Peace, pax, pace, pacem, shalom. Peace co-exists with contentment, inner validation, calm acceptance, and stability. Where one is found, so are the others. Peace denotes a harmonized flow in life, a life lived in deep integrity. To act in any other way would disrupt the experience of peace. Peace offers security in its centeredness.

"Peace is not the absence of conflict, but the presence of God no matter what the conflict."
Peace has to be found within before it can be perceived in the world. In Islam, the inner Jihad is the ego and the Divine will battling for our souls. We have all experienced "will I or won't I?", "should I or shouldn't I"? These are the times our desires fight with our conscience for expression. Anything that is not God's will is the ego talking. Peace comes when we chose to follow the Divine will discerned through authenticity and lived with deep integrity, whether we like it or not, and release our desires, our ego, our fears.

Peaceable people are easily recognized in their openness, their ability to accept others exactly as they are without judgment, while not condoning unacceptable behavior. The experience of peace is a result of surrendering the ego and personal will to the Divine flow we were destined to live. Peace results when we are able to see beyond any situation to the core fears lying beneath and meet another there in vulnerability and love. Peace offers a loving anchor in a chaotic world.

Patience is surrendering to Divine time, not `my time`. It is allied to trust as letting go of `doing` is trust in Divine Will, and patience is reinforcing that trust in knowing what is needed will occur when the time is right, no matter what we might think!

Patience is Divine trust. We may experience restraint, holding back and self control when we are not fully trusting.

Kindness is an extension of our goodwill toward humanity. It is practical, useful and given freely with no expectation of return. Kindness is associated with other qualities such as gentleness, compassion, and sympathy.

Kindness can be a choice. We may choose to act in a kind way even when not feeling it. It can be a conscious step on the spiritual journey. Sometimes, a conscious act of kindness opens the heart for more expressions of kindness. There has been a movement in the last decade or so, groups of people committing to `Random Acts of Kindness". These acts are varied and anonymous, and often result in both parties experiencing positive emotions, the giver from giving and the receiver from being seen and heard by another. The receiver has their existence and needs acknowledged.

The Bible guides us to live, "In purity, understanding, patience, kindness, truthful speech and sincere love". Being kind is part and parcel of treating other humans by the golden rule.

Faithfulness, or fidelity as it is sometimes called, is what commitment is all about, focusing one's attention on upholding any promises and vows made. If we are unable to honour our promises, they are as straws in the wind. This is perhaps one of the most challenging aspects of life. In human relationships, marriage is one of the most important vows a person ever makes. The spouses commit to one another in totality. They provide a chalice in which each can explore themselves and grow, knowing and trusting the other to always be there. Yet there are times in each marriage that challenge. How hard it can be to honour a commitment when all parts of your being want to run away, to escape. It is not always easy to trust another person, to trust them to be honest with you, to be able to hold the space for you when you are kicking off, as it is equally tough to be there in the same way for them. Yet this is what the sacred vow of marriage is all about.

Gentleness is openness and compassion towards others, and can be turned inwards when engaged in self-reflection. Gentleness is the action of humility. Humility is a result of faithfulness. When we focus wholly on the Divine we surrender our ego to trust the Divine voice within. This voice leads us toward the Higher Good, for self and humanity. Gentleness is our expression of humility, of trusting. It is in gentleness that we forgive others. The Course in Miracles says `in your vulnerability your strength lies.` Humility is lauded as the precursor to untold riches of the soul, such as contentment and peace.

Through humility and gentleness we may acquire self control. Once holding fast to the inner belief in God, we invite the Divine within to guide our thoughts and behaviours, this is genuine Self –control as we have handed over ego to our higher inner authority. Our God-self is in control. Egoic self-control doesn't last, it comes in fits and starts as the ego struggles to win and yet in winning is killing its host, so losing and starting to repeat the cycle once more.
Genuine self-control emanates from the indwelling Divine. As we allow the inherent Divine more and more expression, it will emerge in every word and action including self-discipline to guide us into the best we can be. Reigning in the wild excesses of the ego is a step toward freedom. It could be said that gentleness is greater than brute force.
Tao Te Ching says the softest thing in the universe overcomes the hardest thing, this is reminiscent of the channels and shapes that water carves in rock over centuries of flowing in a certain way.

Deep contentment is linked to where we spend our time in our mind. Do we live in the past, chewing over and fermenting injustices? Do we spend our life projecting the pain of the past on to a future that may not happen? Most people do this to some degree or another. Rather than resolve issues as they arise, we sometimes stash the issue away in some emotional pocket, building up a huge backlog of grievances , salivated over by staying in the past and being `right`.

Time, as the fourth dimension, is a construct of man's need for logic and order. There is, in truth, no such thing as past and present, there is only now. It is said that in each moment, all of eternity plays out its existence, experienced as linear time *by the observer*. That this is it. Here. Now. No past, no future, just the deliciousness of living fully alive in the here and now, the present. Being fully present when with others, mentally, emotionally and physically.

We have all been with someone and only half listened. The other half of the brain is working out what to make for dinner, what to say in reply, the shopping list, or the contract at work… it matters not where the mind has gone, it is its absence that diminishes the power of the connection with the other. We have lost the golden opportunity to meet and merge. The distracted mind is seen in anxieties of the future, guilt, reliving the past, resisting change, all of which serve as distraction.

A sense of timelessness could be the gift of being fully present. The past has happened, the future is yet to manifest. Release and be here now. All the fruits of the spirit offer us places to explore with patients and clients, to indicate where they are out of the present moment. Our job is to see where they anchor themselves and to identify the chains that limit their freedom. Deepak Chopra speaks of time being a vehicle for evolution. An evolution denotes growth, movement and change. When we stay in the past we freeze at that place. Bodies will continue to age, minds continue to learn but emotionally there can be stagnation. Growth happens in this very moment. It is an expression of awareness, of being awake to life and not sleepwalking through. Living in the moment, life is eternal, it only becomes something to be chased after or avoided when living in the past or future. Simple presence is respectful and validates the receiver.

Wittgenstein is reputed to have said "if we take eternity to mean not infinite temporal duration but timelessness, eternal life belongs to those who live in the present." What could be a long life is just one witnessed by a conscious observer, someone fully present where time is eternal. Time appears linear when we stay in the pain of the past or dance with the fear of the future. Remember a time when you were lost in something, where your ego had released its tenacious grip and your soul was focused fully in what you were doing? In that experience of timelessness, you had lost conscious awareness of self and merged with the present moment in complete -`beingness`. What if we only `age` when living in the past or future? What if living fully in the present moment stops us from ageing?

Vital Force
"Linking body and soul is the Vital Force" as American Homoeopath JT Kent said in the nineteenth century. The Vital Force is a word homoeopaths use to speak of the life affirming energy that the healing dynamic utilizes. In other modalities it is also known as Chi or Qi.

Dr Kent wrote that the vital force is vice regent to the soul. The soul could be understood as the indwelling, invisible, umbilical cord pulsing with our Divine link, the Vital Force. The soul is understood to be the spiritual, eternal part of humanity. It is the part of us that houses moral beliefs, the inner witness and all aspects of us that relate to love and unity.
The word soul is used in so many connotations, from food to music. In every case soul or soulful takes us to a deep emotional heartfelt place. It is music that transcends words, food that is ambrosia to the gods, sights that stir us beyond emotion.

If mindfulness is focusing the mind, i.e. paying attention, then soulfulness takes this further and becomes total absorption. The underlying reality of soulfulness is pure potential, the meeting point of God and our experience of awe and wonder can be called the soul.

Beauty feeds the soul. Many people find it in nature, in sunsets, in music. Beauty invites us out of this reality to a transcendent place beyond logic. It invites contemplation and at the same time, when we are in awe we lose a sense of ourselves as separate. Beauty can be a portal to Divine union.

Thomas Merton said "Soul is revealed in attachment, love, and community, as well as in retreat on behalf of inner communing and intimacy." His poetry gives words to the unspeakable awe with which he regarded life. He said "This is the goal of the souls path - to feel existence: not to overcome life's struggles and anxieties, but to know life first hand, to exist fully in context." He appreciates the error in placing judgments of good or bad on any experience.

The second we buy into our experiences and give them a judgment value we have stepped back into separation and ego. This is not the soul's path. The soul's path is to take us back to freedom and it finds so many delightful ways to do so. The soul craves time in natural beauty on a regular basis, time to stop and be absorbed back into the glorious universe, time to reconnect with the Divine both outside and within.

Wistfulness and yearning are soul words as they depict the emotions behind our unconscious pull to beauty. The power the colours, shapes, images and flow have on us is beyond words, it is indeed `soulful'. If we are deprived of beauty it affects us; it is a form of torture as much as denying our bodies of food or water. We need beauty to feed the soul without it we atrophy, our heart and soul is removed from life leaving us husks of bodies. Mother Theresa said "The real hunger in the western world is the hunger for the soul. "

No matter how much we have materially, without soul we are as psychopaths in our disconnection. Richard Rohr said "The soul needs meaning as much as the body needs food." Currently in the western world it could be argued that our souls are being starved as junk food is offered as sustenance.

As we are considering the ultimate definition of health we can see here that a living connection with our soul is a profound part of this description. Perfect health is when we are in deep alignment with our soul. Awareness of this is crucial in establishing a healthy body, and a healthy life.

Jung spoke of Self being the fulcrum of action and intelligence that feels both the weight of the soul and the intellect. He referred to it as `transcendent function`. If the aim for integration and alignment in the depths of humankind results in the fruits of the spirit, we experience them in fulfilling work and rewarding relationships, the strength of vulnerability and better health.

In our spiritual journey we strive for consciousness and awareness. We strive to live the qualities of our highest values. In our soul we experience the fruits of this search, the pleasure and pain of all emotions and experiences on the journey. Thomas Merton said, "The ultimate marriage of spirit and soul, animus and anima, is the wedding of heaven and earth, our highest ideals and ambitions united with our lowliest symptoms and complaints." Herein dwells the Mystic-Healer.

To make this section personally useful and more tangible, what is your exact definition of health?

Spend time focusing on your own precise definition to give you a stable anchor to support clarity in your practice. Well attended to, it can be a yardstick to evaluate all you do and offer, including treatments, ancillary advice or your way of connection. Yearly revisiting of your definition of health is encouraged. As you grow in your self awareness, your definition grows as well. It is a dynamic living process.

Your definition of health paints a beautiful picture, a portrait of humanity in its divinity, a place where we all, consciously or unconsciously, yearn to reside. The Divine in infinite gnosis gave us a perfect gift, the help we need to find our way home. If at first we don't listen, the gift gets larger, bigger, 'noisier' until we acknowledge it. Then and only then can we turn in the direction of peace and Divine living. We have mistaken the wonder of this gift and called it sickness.

"Someday, after we have mastered the winds, the waves, the tides and gravity,
we shall harness for God the energies of love.
Then for the second time in the history of the world,
we will have discovered fire."
Pierre Teilhard de Chardin

Sickness

Where sickness comes from
Having an experiential definition of health offers a clear goal for the evaluation of symptoms. If health is a deep connection with the Divine and alignment with our core mission, then everything else is an expression of our separation from these. Every historical tradition has a story around the separation. For example, in Christianity it comes from the time we chose the apple. One interpretation of what this choice represents is a choice to believe our reason gifted mind absolutely over the heartfelt, invisible, intuitive dynamic connection we had previously enjoyed with our Higher Power. In pursuing knowledge to the exclusion of intuition, we lose trust in the small, still voice within. When we disconnect at this deep level, we cut our umbilical cord to the Divine and then our energies have no way to be `charged up`. There is no genuine power supply. This loss of energy eventually leads to illness.

This separation from the Divine is being played out in the secular world as relationships break down and crumble. Families are being torn apart by disconnected relationships, shattering adults and destroying children. Children need emotional input as much as they need food, water and air. It would seem that we are moving into a generation of physically fully grown, often very well educated people, who are sadly emotionally young and unprepared for mature relationship They replay the cycle of attraction and disconnection once again. They are not resourced by parents who have taught them by example how to integrate intellect with deep listening to the heart.

Fear of being alone is a deep seated fear of separation. In every age and era, there have been ways to distract ourselves from our fears. Currently, chatter on mobile phones, texts, twitter and all other manner of perpetual communication, talking much but saying nothing, immersed in the delusion of connection are common avoidance tactics. The scary silence is tempered by the beeps and whistles of modern technology.

Separation from the Divine is culminating in an epidemic of lonely people. Solitary confinement is an acknowledged form of torture for prisoners, it is the ultimate state of separation. Isolation is the worst human suffering. Even in monasteries and convents, the monks and nuns live communally. For a very few deeply committed men and women, there are hermitages in which to be alone. These are people with a deep sense of the aliveness of the Divine, with a daily breathing relationship with the Divine and great awareness of the world as it is. There are few people so deeply aligned as to be fully comfortable alone, the vast majority of us need each other.

Connection to the Divine is the meaning of life. Once all the paths of distraction have been exhausted, what else is there?

Separation from the Divine can lead to loss of the awe and wonder of the natural world and of life itself. It is a black hole of meaninglessness that results in ennui at best, and suicidal thoughts or actions at worst. This loss of God insidiously erodes our sense of worth, our mission, our purpose and our memory of who we really are. The end result is some form of illness.

As Mystic-Healers this is what we are addressing, a manifestation of symptoms that emerge from loneliness, the disconnection from the Divine and from our sense of purpose.

Many people focus on their physical ailments, unaware that what they really need is an in depth conversation on the bigger questions of life. The more we know of the core of illness, the more we can guide them in the direction needed, we can point them back to their God. The question is how does each of us perceive our `god`?

Personal Belief

Since our beliefs become our bodies, it is essential that we regularly update them with our accumulated learning and experience. It is important to take time to hit the refresh key. If we don't, we run the risk of living life under a god who is external to us.

It is said that a person's behavior tells you their definition of the Divine. If they are judgmental, then their God is a judgmental God. If they are vengeful, then that is how they understand the Divine to be. If they are forgiving, their God is a forgiving one; if they are loving, then their God is a loving one; if they are compassionate, it equates to a compassionate Higher Power.

Equally, people who have no conscious connection to any sense of a Higher Power will still worship an idol. It might be a football team, a sport, a fashion, or a pop group. They may worship being right, gossip, scandal, being admired, having power or knowing the most. The range of idols is vast. Humanity throws in its lot by believing in the reality of the unreal. The Course in Miracles tells us that there is either love or fear. If something is not love, a joining and merging into unity, then it is fear.

In this fear people live half-lives, working, eating, sleeping - all for what? Without a modus operandi, life is existence to be `got through`.

Our illnesses reflect the beliefs we hold. An obese person might come with diabetes. What point is there in treating the diabetes without exploring the role food is playing in their life? What is behind their eating? It might be a belief that there is never enough, it might be a form of hiding, avoiding intimacy, or a protection from some pain in the past. The issue is not the obesity, but what is behind it. Regard yourself as a medical detective and keep asking `why? Dive in and ferret around until the person discerns the truth of their world view. Then and only then is change possible. Until then we are moving symptoms around, palliating at best and suppressing at worst. Nothing we

33

`do` to another has any effect at all. Only when they `experience` the truth of their world view can they release it; thus allowing an updated view of 'God' to unfold.

It cannot be highlighted enough how important this is, as everything we think, say or do comes from the level of our belief.

When choosing to see a practitioner of any kind, it is good to bear in mind that the limitations of their beliefs determine how far along the path of healing they can take you.
We cannot take our clients any deeper into self-awareness than we are personally willing to go ourselves. That might be our only responsibility, to be open to expanding self-awareness.

Rationality
The disintegration of humanity commenced with the shift from a perspective held in tune with the intuitive indwelling Divine to one based on a reliance on external forces. We began to believe in the supremacy of `man` and his knowledge. As the centuries went by, science tightened its grip even more and we began to believe only what we could see, hear, touch, quantify. How do you measure God? What does the soul weigh? The madness in this concept is clear the second these questions are asked, yet much of the western world has stepped into the place of believing and trusting science over their innate connection. When we trust in our desire for knowledge and override our innate gnosis, we split within causing all manner of energetic illnesses to manifest. It is through this internal Grand Canyon that illnesses emerge. They drain energy, hope and joy leaving us battling depression, tiredness, and ennui.

The ego fights an eternal internal fight for supremacy with the soul. It is here, in the inner dwelling of humanity that duality is confronted. It is here that the choices are made in every decision on a moment by moment basis. Until there is internal peace, there will be no peace externally. All the traditions impart the wisdom, "what is within, is mirrored outwith".

External validation

It is easy to see what a person believes by observing how they behave. Everyone has a belief that drives their behaviour. For some, it is the journey with their Higher Power. For most, the main belief driving them is fear. Their behavior reflects their desire to palliate their fear in every way.

Who do you want to please, whose opinion matters to you? Whose authority do you submit to? Who gives you permission, and in whom do you believe without question?

When we externally validate, we risk losing our true self, we dis-honour the truth of who we are. Herein lies the source of pain. Another human being is guaranteed to let us down, no matter how much they love or care about us. Valuing ourselves solely as perceived by others equates to a shell of a person, a husk of humanity that flails around constantly looking for someone to tell them what to do, think, and be. In its most extreme manifestation, it could be described as a form of an emotional leech.

Equally, the need for validation through an external source such as attracting a partner, winning a race, getting a promotion, etc. is empty. Once it is achieved, the fears creep in again and the pursuit recommences. Those who validate through relationships will move on to the next conquest, the competitors will find the next race or promotion as the ego, once gratified, allows only a brief spell of ease before stimulating doubt, fear and insecurity once again.

Ultimately though, the day comes when the attractiveness lessens, the competitors are younger and fitter, the ceiling, glass or otherwise, is reached. The only way forward is the great void within. The classic mid-life crisis could be one example of this. Awakening to the internal validation of who we really are and what motivates us is essential. This is why it is so helpful to ask patients and clients what they wanted to be in their teens, before they were told they couldn't do it, for whatever reason. This youthful passion is the direct line to their mission. It is the physical location of their sense of `home`, of belonging.

A major risk of validating externally is the pressure it projects onto another. If their view is what frames you, then you exist at the whim of their moods. Maybe they are aware of how much you use them, how you determine who you are based on their experience of you but what happens when they have a less than positive day? Are you able to self-validate enough to get over it, or do you go down with them? If the energy source you have existed on is closed off, you may feel abandoned, or find yourself in rage and angry projection of the other's behaviour. Depending how much validation the other offered, it can be a wakeup call to `own` yourself and take responsibility. If a great deal has been placed on the other, then it may result in a sense of devastation, the ego decimated and fragmented.

The opinions of others we cherish and need so much in external validation is actually given to us through the lens of the others perception. Who are they judging or applauding? Us? Themselves? Their own shadows? This introduces the ego in all its glory as our shadow side.

Ego, as used in the ancient Greek, meaning small separate self. It is the part of us that wants us to remain special, the part within that decides to trust our desires rather than discern and adhere to the Will of the Divine.

The ego is the part that feels unloved, alone, rejected, abandoned. It is here that shame and pride exist hand in hand, hiding in the shadows, threatening us with exposure if challenged.

It is ego that competes to become the best and win so others see us as special, but the second we become special, we are also separate from them. The very specialness we craved lands us in the jail of isolation.

The ego is the greatest conman of them all. If, as discussed before, unity, love and community is the ultimate aim of living, then the ego goes along with us and says, yes, you can belong, just get another exam, lose weight, get the right house/car/job etc. Effectively it `agrees` with our intention to go home to God, but it distracts us into focusing on ourselves and thus keeps us separate. It's cunning grows in its wiliness as our self-awareness expands.

The ego measures things, it is the part of us that counts all we give and expects equal return. Fear of lacking comes from ego. The ego believes in limitations and scarcity, the soul in abundance of joy.

The Course in Miracles says "Are you Host to God, or hostage to the ego" How much time each day is spent as hostage and how much hosting the Divine? This is the journey of the Mystic-Healer: to spend more and more time each day as host to God.

For many of us, each time we open our mouths the ego falls out. Each time we see our ego in action we have the opportunity to choose. In transcending the small `ego-self`, one discovers the `God-Self`. Each time the choice is for God there is a deep sense of relief, a peace in the freedom that Love offers.

Deepak Chopra sums it up beautifully when he says, "Choiceless awareness is another name for free awareness. By freeing up the choice maker inside, you reclaim your right to live without boundaries, acting on the Will of God with complete trust."

There is no judiciary in the world that is as harsh and cruel as the inner judge, the ego. Marianne Williamson says "the ego both sets us up to do the wrong thing then punishes us savagely for having done so." Diets offer the perfect example here, the ego tempts and teases us towards something we know we shouldn't have, then when we succumb, it beats us soundly with guilt and shame.

When we understand that a person is acting from their ego, we have a window into their fears. This is a powerful tool to jimmy open the safe that contains their heart and freedom. Health arises from dissolved fear, projection and blame, allowing genuine, deep, heartfelt love to flow unhindered. Releasing belief in the ego, focusing less on others imperfections and being compassionate with our own reduces the ego's power over us. The ego ups the ante as we focus more and more on our relationship with the Divine. It is the ultimate manipulator.

The ego fights all attempts to open to Divine love, making it difficult to sustain a spiritual practice. We simply forget how the ego distracts us. The ego is most scared of unconditional love. Unconditional love is releasing the delusion of separation and loving the other as the Higher Self. It is quite interesting to see how many people are passionate for connection, desperate to have a partner yet terrified of the depth or openness and trust that this entails.

We see many people who have serial relationships, meeting, merging and melding for the first few years, then when the love starts to shift from lust to a deeper more intimate place, fear and vulnerability creep into the equation. Rather than open yet further to their partner and risk even greater intimacy and vulnerability, they will back off, find another relationship and commence the cycle again. When lust masquerades as love and sex as intimacy, a relationship is built on sand and is destined to be washed away in the tsunami of seemingly exciting new people and experiences.

Despite the conscious desire to belong, we have an internal unconscious saboteur getting us to focus on a small part of ourselves to avoid the loss of the ego that the total merging of the soul with another results in. Merging the soul with another takes real intimacy, which is deeply scary. Human beings thrive when they are seen, heard and held in unconditional love and acceptance. Yet we often fear being seen. When we are seen, we may be rejected, deemed not good enough.

The Shadow
A term coined last century naming the parts of our inner world that we dislike and would prefer not to have! In truth the shadow side is neither good nor bad. The value of each aspect is what each of us ascribes to it, hence we all describe the shadow differently based on our susceptibilities and fears.

Invariably, the shadow side refers to the aspects of ourselves that we have judged as negative traits. These are the areas we judge others on. For example, should a practitioner with low self-esteem have a session with a client of healthy self-esteem, the practitioner, in their perception of themselves as normal, might well note that the client is arrogant. Being self-aware is just the start, we have to assess ourselves against the highest values we can. Our beliefs become the benchmark for evaluation.

Understanding the continuum of self awareness is helpful as it is normally accepted that what we judge someone else on is something that we are denying within ourselves. In the situation above, it is not that we are suppressing arrogance, but living in false humility. It is the polar aspect of the same continuum, arrogance manifesting as false humility. The other person rankles us as we resent their ability to behave more honestly. In this situation, it is the falseness that is the issue.

Once we stop judging others we are more able to accept the truth of who we really are. This is to say to the client, thank you for reflecting me, for being me, for opening me to the wonder and expanse of my inner self! This doesn't mean we dive into arrogance or anger, but that we accept it as part of who we are. We can choose how to `be` in a more expansive way and place our need to show up in this manner in a greater context. The conundrum here is that we have to be self-aware before we can confront and accept the inner demons. This is a deeply scary place. For most, it takes a fear, event, situation or experience much greater than the fears we currently hold to propel us into the inward journey.

The spiritual journey is opening ourselves to the `all` of humanity. It is a step through fear toward the unity with all and the in-dwelling Divine. The fears that surround this portal to God come from the ego, that part of ourselves that is desperate to be special and separate. The innermost part is our Highest Self, pure unconditional love. Duality comes from the small, still voice of God (Higher self) being drowned out by the screams, rants and rages of the ego demanding its way.

In opening to the shadow side, we are uniting ourselves in the most perfect loving way. Our partner brings up our shadow side for us in all the things they do that create friction. These are gifts that if we choose to accept, will support the inner journey towards self-knowledge and acceptance, which leads us into peace.

The success of a relationship is dependent on the ability of the individuals to be in integrity and authenticity with one another, communicate, remain open hearted and truly accept the relationship as it is.

It is from the intensity of the emotion in a relationship that we gain the most: be it someone we love who reminds us of who we really are at our best, or our enemies who reflect back our deepest fears and challenges. Each brings a reflection and both are true. One we welcome and one we resist, yet both are judgments. Both are the same; mirrors of who we are. When we reject our shadow side, we distort the truth around it and project it onto another. By denying it, the inner ego kids us that we are perfect.

The light of consciousness within defuses the power of the shadow once the judgments have been released, transformation happens. Utter alchemy!

Perception

As previously discussed, world view determines actions in accordance with beliefs. It is invariably people's view of the world that is causing pain and anguish. Reconnecting with divine alignment is where true healing occurs.

No medicine or therapy can change the past, but it can change the way it is remembered. Assisting someone to change their mind is a miracle. During a follow on appointment, a client may relate a tale of a situation arising that reminded them of an event many years earlier, only this time they addressed it differently. This different way of seeing, deep inner acceptance and willingness to release attachment to the memory can be very powerful. What was once seen as a tragedy, may repeat as a comedy.

I recall many years ago being asked by a long time dear friend about my childhood. Well, I got ready, first a large glass of water and then a box of Kleenex as I prepared myself for the habitual memories I had formed decades earlier. I was, in full flow, weeping and a wailing and `poor little me-ing` when the phone rang and my friend went to answer it. I had ten minutes to sit with it. When my friend returned, I shook my head and said, no, that wasn't it, my childhood was fine, it gave me the opportunities I needed to be the person I am today for which I am so grateful.

In that moment I understood how the perception of the past can be changed. I stopped long enough to look at it from a place of being centered in the present and was able to see a different truth of how it had been. This allowed the memories to dissolve away as my present mindset was able to perceive it differently. I was left with a huge realization of how much our mindset affects everything we do and how a shift in perception allows us to see things differently. Choosing love over ego trusts in the bigger picture, even if we can't see it at that moment in time.

The world continually provides us with situations that reinforce our perception of the world and our place in it. It becomes a catch twenty two. I remember a girl at school with very low self-esteem, she felt she wasn't worth much and everyone would leave her. The guy she liked asked her out and for a brief while she was happy. Then she began to push him away, she pushed and pushed in her behavior until he ended the relationship at which point, amidst the sadness of loss was a quiet, smug satisfaction that she had been right. She had been left again, thus validating her low self-esteem. She had created a situation to collude with her self perception. This is reminiscent of Groucho Marks who is reputed to have said that he wouldn't be a member of a club who would have him as a member!

Quantum physics concurs. It has been proven that the observer alters the outcome; how in fact, the result is directly linked to the world view of the observer. This is exciting as it confirms that we can indeed change our lives, our world. It reaffirms the power of humanity and our role as co-creator with the Divine.

This could be seen as our true place of power in the world, creating the reality we want. Our thoughts precede anything and everything material in the world, so we create a world that is the self fulfilling prophecy of our active delusion. The world we experience exists in response to our perceptions, it is the aftereffect of our world view.

The block in healing is our perception. Our worldview is the impediment to healing, it is as simple as that. In practice, discerning a client's or patient's worldview is essential in helping them to identify the blocks that limit their healing.

Our world view is found in the cumulation of our fears and judgments. Our health, as well as the material circumstances that surround us, are a manifestation of fear and judgment. Our goal, therefore, is the removal of fear and judgment, allowing a greater worldview, one free from our subjective interpretation.

The hub of the wheel is the truth and each of us are different spokes, each spoke extends out until it meets the rim and each spoke ends on a different part of the rim depending on the perception. We can use the perceived reality as signposts to the inner state.

Attachment

The Buddha spoke much of attachment being the source of humanity's suffering. Our attachment to some thing, person, or belief has with it a rigidity. We have ascribed this `other` with a value and that denotes our investment in it. Love freely given is the gift of God. Most love that is given is conditional and dependent on certain criteria being attained. When we love freely, we are not attached to anyone or anything, nor to views or beliefs. It is when we are attached and have given meaning to things that we step into fear, allowing possessions or others to have power over us. In this acquisition of power we have lost the capacity for blessed peace. We fear loss.

Attachment has many forms. Its most extreme expression is addiction. We might be very attached to being right, or to being in control, or to being in a co-dependent relationship with another person. It could be an image we are attached to, behaving in a way commensurate with our desire for others to view us in a particular way. Consider the number of people in music or on screen who reinvent themselves to attract another section of public adoration. For some of these people, it is attachment to validation through others that is their motivation. When we discover what the client or patient is attached to, we find the area that needs to be addressed.

We all have negative feelings. The art is not to believe them, but to use them as indicators of attachment. The pain they cause gains our attention, whilst offering us a signpost to the Divine within if we find a way to transmute them. Jealousy, for example, could be the flame to ignite the passion within, to `up` our game, as well as tear us up emotionally. When we are frozen in the experience of emotions, we have problems. Life is a fluid flowing dynamic to which a healthy response is equally fluid and flowing. Life happens to us, it is how we deal with it that defines us, and how we personalize it. How much is based on ego and how much on love?

Suffering
When we attach to being 'right', to being the best, the most beautiful, intelligent, cleverest, most perfect etc., we suffer. One of the reasons for suffering is that once we have achieved the desired pinnacle in whatever way, the only way is down or striving to sustain this place. This means investing huge amounts of time and/or money into retaining the desired state.The Buddha spoke of attachment being the source of suffering. It doesn't matter what the object is, the verb is 'attach', meaning being invested in relationship with the object. It might be envy or jealousy, or an inferiority complex disguised as arrogance, anything that the ego had determined is worthy. Hmm, ego, again, it does get about a bit! We attach to the characteristic which our ego has determined validates us. If it is being the best at something, then our whole life is spent ensuring that we are. The anguish in discovering we are not is unbearable. It might be finding out we are wrong or feeling rejected.

Physical pain can seem much easier to deal with, it hurts, we scream or cry, and release endorphins that reduce the pain. The pain goes when the underlying source is addressed. With ego pain, the feeling stays. It needs to be fed either by sharing relentlessly with another, or by being palliated repeatedly, as the soothing effects of palliation wear off quickly. Attachment leads to illness. The negative feelings triggered from unrequited desires erode the compassion that dwells in the heart.

When we believe that the object of our attachment is real we suffer. The pain of suffering, the attachment, is all in our minds. In theory, we only have to change our mind, and we would be well. For many people, suffering is essential as it validates their existence. They only feel alive when they feel physical or mental/emotional pain. If we exist only in relation to our desires, then only when we are emoting are we alive. Ego desires are black voids for energy, they suck you dry, they suck your friends dry. They exhaust all in the process.

Stop for a nanosecond, be fully in the present moment and see how much pain is there. Very likely there is little or no pain. Bring the past or future back into mind and experience the pain again. Explore the underlying cause of attachment, based on a fear. Release the fear and be free. So easy to write, and so hard to do. Our fears come from the deepest of places and represent our distrust in anything `higher` than humanity.

The western worldview colludes with the ego desires by asserting each individual's right to be free from pain, and encourages instant gratification.

Illusion

Einstein said, "A human being is part of the whole, called by us, 'Universe', a part limited in time and space. He experiences himself, his thoughts and feelings as something separate from the rest - a kind of optical delusion of his consciousness. This delusion is a kind of prison for us, restricting us to our personal desires and to affection for a few persons nearest us. Our task must be to free ourselves from this "prison." " This resonates with an enhanced definition of health as it describes in detail the chains that bind us. These chains are what the Mystic-Healer is committed to dissolving, opening the way for freedom.

Illusion and delusion both refer to a belief in something that is not true, which comes from the ego (fear), and exerts a great deal of authority over us. Most of us remain imprisoned by it. Many traditions speak of the illusion of the world, how it is unreal and moveable like the mists of Avalon that only clear to allow the viewer to see Avalon when their mind is open to it. If we chose to think as God does, then all we see, give and receive will be the Love that is the Divine. If, however, we choose thoughts of lacking or loss, abandonment and separation is what we will see in every situation.

The Course in Miracles is based around the precept.
"Nothing unreal exists.
Nothing real can be threatened.
Therein lies the peace of God."
This sums it up. If the only real thing is love, then that is all that matters, the rest of the narrative of your life's story exists only in your mind.

There was a teenage serial drama on television a few years ago, called `Buffy the vampire Slayer`. Buffy, a main character, takes on, fights and kills the vampires. In one episode, she is seen as being in a psychiatric ward with her parents and a doctor as she dances between the two worlds. One depiction of her was of being a high school girl in the hospital, the other was of her as a vampire slayer. It highlighted the seeming reality of both versions of her, which is the dream and which the reality? Most of us have experienced a dream where we wake in the dream except we then find we are still in the dream….and eventually waken into this, the waking dream!

The aim of healing is to bring to conscious awareness, to wake up to the experience of the indwelling Divine and allow it to transform our world view. When this happens, our perceptions soften becoming more gentle and less fear and judgment based, moving us into deeper community with one another. This takes courage, huge courage, as it requires us to look where we have dared not look, to dive in where we are unsure of the water's depth. It sounds just like the aggravation of the homoeopathic remedy. In both cases, the healing comes from the experiential, not the intellectual. The mind is the place that births delusion and a problem is never healed at the place where it originated.

Meditation is a powerful tool. It takes us deep within, beyond the immediate consciousness relating to the outside world to the small, still voice within that holds the truth of who we are. Contemplation offers the opportunity to dissolve illusions.

Expectations

We could look at an expectation as a disappointment waiting to happen. Expectations of self can result in fulfilling a self-determined inadequacy that then becomes a prophecy. Expectations of others are disguised judgments. We judge based on our expectations. In both cases, we are not holding either our self or the other in deep acceptance. We have pre-defined what we think they should be, do or achieve. Where is the love in that? The moment we assume to know anything for another we have stepped into separation and the illusion that we know better for them. From here it is an easy step into control and fixing, an area those of us working in health care need to be aware of. Expectations come from the ego.

Expectations don't just limit how we see our self or others, but also how we receive from others. From `I am not worthy`, to, ` is this all I am worth?` Each one of us has an unconscious worth and we cross this line at our peril. Much like the dieter who achieves their weight loss yet it is just a matter of time before the weight is regained. We cannot sustain greater feelings of self-worth than we unconsciously believe to be true.

Incongruence

All of life is energy; all vibrations and frequencies are energy It is pivotal to health that energies flow collectively, moving together like a murmur of starlings or geese, with the collective moving all as one.

If we attempt to serve two opposing masters, there will likely be misery and discord, frequently manifesting in illness. What the body cannot reconcile, it will stash event by event, accruing in cells and organs until such time as there is overload. Disease and pain are the expression of the build up.

Consider the many headaches, insomnia, coughs and colds that chunter through life, upsetting enough, yet not seriously in need of addressing. They can be viewed as the little warning lights of a car when some function or another is not working properly. These minor ailments are indicative of a loss of integrity, indicating a place where compromise has split the divine flow of energy resulting in fragmentation.

In large companies, the soul of an individual can be disrupted by having to adhere to someone else's vision for success or by the integrity of the organization being lesser than the individual working there. This dissonance opens the way for potentially more serious symptoms.

Similarly, on any given day, seemingly minor events can open the way for illness as a result of the inner clash between integrity and ego. Behaving counter to our inner belief results in dissonance, this manifests physically. It is impossible to hold opposing views without some fall out somewhere inside.

No matter what we do, how `good` our actions are, the effect is muted if it is at odds with what we truly believe. When there is congruence, the power becomes ten times what is humanly possible. There are many tales of parents lifting cars off their children etc. Their only goal is to remove the car from their child. They have one focus uniting all thoughts and actions in perfect alignment, resulting in strength that is powerful beyond reality. Might this power be our natural state when we live in complete integrity?

Honouring and speaking from a deep inner truth results in a laser beam of power. When we are out of alignment we are diffused like a 20 watt bulb, able to see the outlines, but not able to read the fine print.

Incongruence is often experienced as emotional dissonance, resulting in either a state of chronic indecision or a rash choice that is tightly held. Again we return to the value of clarity in one's inner beliefs, discernment creates a chalice to support everything we do.

Humiliation
Shame is one of the most powerful influences on of the western world. Underpinning the socially acceptable drive for perfection

is the deeply unacceptable fear of humiliation, of being shamed. Many a life is lived with secrecy. Humility is one of the 'side effects' of the spiritual journey, it denotes a place of deep self-acceptance, of knowing yourself in relation to God, the universe, to the world, to others and to self. Many people live in a state of false humility, which, by very definition is not humility at all but a form of inverted arrogance. The truly humble person is being fully themselves which may well be to be great and known by many, or not! Humility is acceptance of the gifts with which the Divine has blessed you, and bringing them fully into 'be-ing' in the world. Neither falsely promoting oneself, nor denying one's gifts.

In a USA study a decade ago, people working for the Fortune 500 companies were questioned around their fears. As expected, fear of death emerged as the primary fear. The next most named fear was a fear of being found out, which came as a surprise to the researchers. People fear others seeing the 'truth' of who they really are. In as goal orientated a society as the west is today, we are judged on what we do and know, not who we are. This dehumanises us to the level of robots, while fear ties us into the system, denying our true inner being.

The fear of being found out is a fear of being humiliated, about being exposed as a fraud in some way, not as good/clever/pretty/etc. as you would have others believe. Each one of us has this fear lurking deep within around some aspect or other of our lives.

The energy it takes to deny the truth of who we are to this extent becomes greater and greater as the lies of life compound our denial, draining energy away from creativity in all its forms to keep a 'lid on it'. As the energy is misdirected over time, we use more coping strategies that afford a temporary high, a brief escape from the energy drain of denial, such as stimulants and shopping. Eventually this doesn't work either and the body begins to break down in its attempt to keep the mind safe, to keep the secret hidden.

As anyone who has ever opened up and finally revealed a `secret` to a Mystic-Healer knows, the relief is tremendous. The world did not stop revolving, the listener did not turn away in disgust, and, often, sharing the secret diffuses the shame and the person is left wondering why they had held onto it for so long.

Shame is in the mindset of the person. Many years ago a friend planned to meet me as she had something she wanted to tell me. We met and had lunch and I listened intently so as to be supportive and nothing was mentioned. Eventually I asked her what it was she had wanted to tell me. She replied that she had told me three times that she was gay but I wasn't listening. I was listening but to me and my belief system, there is no shame or need for secrecy around homosexuality, so it did not compute. This encounter highlighted that not only do we have secrets and shames, but that everyone denotes a different situation as a shame or worthy of secrecy.

The Course in Miracles says ` vulnerability is our greatest strength`. How sweetly and gently true this is, having the vulnerability to release fear and embrace humility results in finding freedom, the greatest strength we can choose.

It is sad that invariably the shame and fear of humiliation are around being ourselves, that our being-ness is not enough. This is one interpretation of the fall from the Garden of Eden. Adam and Eve stopped focussing on God and focused on themselves, and therein lay shame. God consciousness is total unity and a gnosis of one's true self, anything less is a denial of the truth, the truth that animates life. This is one of the greatest barriers to inner healing.

Barriers to Inner Healing
From the moment we turn our focus away from God we reject ourselves. Falsehoods vibrate differently, the perfect flow is disrupted, the eye of the hurricane is lost.

Rather than recognize this, repent and re-enter the ` kingdom of heaven`, this place of peace, our eyes close and the struggle of humanity commences as we try in vain to recreate heaven on earth. How simple it could be to stand before our Divine Being and say I am sorry, I lost my way and now I am returned, to once again experience the bliss of heaven, the peace that surpasses all understanding. But no, we frequently choose to stay in pain. When we resist surrender and humility, any ownership of a mistake is projected out-with and onto others whom we then chose not to forgive. In truth, we are not forgiving ourselves, preferring to wallow in the guilt that crucifies us.

We tie ourselves into the pain of life through invisible bonds. The ultimate bondage situation is in our minds. The key to freedom is in our hands. Our free will offers us escape, but will we take it? Herein lies the power of fear: of change, of potentiality, of freedom. Freedom to be the Divine child of the universe we really are.

Bearing all this in mind it is easy to see how the Mystic-Healer has to be gentle, non judgmental and compassionate with everyone to allow them the freedom to truly open up.
"Our wounds are the only thing humbling enough to break our attachment to our false self."
Richard Rohr

Dark night of the soul
Despite the distractions and avoidance techniques, the soul keeps on calling us home. Eventually the ego may run out of ways to distract us, or life throws a curve that the ego cannot answer. The result can be a breakdown which, in many cases, could also be experienced as a breakthrough.

This is seen in energy medicine such as homoeopathy as an `aggravation`. This is where the homoeopathic remedy exaggerates the imbalance, just enough for the self-healing mechanism, the Vital Force, to recognize the reflection mirrored back and to respond therapeutically. The aggravation is where the ego cannot cope anymore and the only way through is to surrender and allow the healing dynamic full expression. The person may phone to say ` I can't take it any more`, `I can't do this anymore`. The use of the `I` demonstrates the ego voice and the surrender into divine healing.

The dark night of the soul is another way to describe this transformative time. It is here that all the egoic links and references, ego beliefs and behaviors melt away leaving the person naked and vulnerable. The experience of which is a truly terrifying place to be, yet once faced, will dissolve opening the way for the Divine to flow and reconnect with the soul.

It is the fear that surrounds this disintegration of the ego that many people spend their lives avoiding. Some might collect possessions or people feeling that if they have enough, they can hang onto the illusion and avoid their inner self. The fear of not existing leads to distracted behavior. It is true, of course, they do not exist, not in the way they currently perceive themselves. The western world lauds the ego and the power and illusion it holds dear. It has also thrown out the baby with the bathwater in a collective rejection of the spiritual world. Secularism places more emphasis on the ego than is healthy, as evidenced by rising levels of suicide, depression and other mental issues. This dark night of the soul is a time when we berate ourselves for past follies and mistakes. Our sins themselves are our punishment. It is when all self-perceptions have fallen away, leaving us naked and screaming in pain with our emotional skin ripped away before it can grow and reform. The dark night is when all that we thought mattered is removed, taken away. The dark night of the soul is the portal between who we thought we were and whom we really are. The dark night is the birthing journey of the soul, a time when you cannot retreat though all is dark around you and suffused by fear of the unknown. Yet once through, just like life after the womb, all is completely different. It reminds me of the caterpillar who, when encased in the chrysalis has to actually dissolve before it can transform into the butterfly.

Middle age is often a time when the veils between the worlds of the divine and of ego are thinner. It offers many potentially life altering crises, from families leaving home or divorce, to releasing fertility, parents dying or reaching and tipping over the pinnacle at work. Middle age is a time where we might stop long enough to review life thus far and are often horrified at how far we are from where we imagined we might be. This can result in guilt and self loathing, and a deep sense of disempowerment, raising many fears to the surface. These are all points of change and as such, offer a clear view of the portal to growth. We cannot grow without change. The pain this brings up may impel us into distraction, however over time, enough of these incidents may happen to force us to look within. If not, we are subsumed into ego chaos and the pain that brings. If we are fortunate, the realization that there must be another way dawns. That, as Gandhi and Einstein are both reputed to have asserted, `a problem cannot be resolved on the same level at which it originated`. When the ego can no longer answer the questions, the seeking begins. The ego has collapsed (or is collapsing) and yet, I am still here. Logically, there must be something greater than ego, something transcendent of the self.

The dark night of the soul is the alchemy of existence. It is the crucible in which our small selves are burned by the fires of pain and recrimination, we either stay in our ego, `right`, and burn up in agony or we surrender that shell of ourselves as a snake releases it's `too-small` skin. The fires of the dark night purify us through the release of the ego. We release the physical senses, logic, reason, knowledge and worldly power to open to the `gnosis` within. We incinerate external validation to validate through divine inner connection. From the ego crying out to be loved, we enter a place where we open to the love that is continually there, and are then able to offer love to everyone and everything allowing love to flow through unimpeded. This, in truth, is the only choice we actually ever make. Every other choice comes from it. Do we choose love or fear in each and every moment?

The dark night of the soul is the portal to divine peace, to a re-alignment of core truths that weave into a harmonious flow in life. From this `breakthrough`, people change. We may change jobs, hobbies, friends or diets, we may change how we spend our free time. We may find solace in quiet. Each small shift builds and reinforces other small shifts, until we become aware that we have stepped beyond depression and feelings of alienation to a slower, simpler, gentler way of being, finally living with less judgement and more peace, and foregoing fear to open to give and receive love, a life of simplicity. There is something definite about this, it is not a choice, we **will** enter into it, the only choice we have is when.

How many times in our culture is this valuable opportunity lost when antidepressants or other palliative substances are offered? Sadly, very frequently, if we use the measure of the sales of such products. Perhaps many people would benefit from support in exploring their nihilism and emerging reborn afterwards.

Marianne Williamson wrote about depression being to the soul what a fever is to the body. Depressive feelings offer an opportunity to burn up negativity allowing health to return. It might be a few days or last a lot longer, "Either way, they are part of a mystical detox of our accumulated fear and despair."

Seven Distractions
St John of the Cross wrote a seminal piece on the Dark Night of the Soul where he explores the Seven Deadly Sins as they depict the inner landscape we live with on a daily basis. These seven facets of fear can be addressed. As with all things, bring awareness to them and immediately they become diminished. On the inner journey, name the fears, apply forgiveness, free your soul, and open to giving and receiving love.

- *Pride*, holding a high or inordinate opinion of one's own dignity, importance, merit, or superiority, is ego in full play. Pride is believing in our ego over the indwelling God.

- *Avarice* seeks to control life through an insatiable greed for riches, a miserly desire to gain and hoard wealth.

- *Luxury* craves indulgent extras in life, needs have given way to greeds and the person has more than they could ever need.

- *Wrath* is projection of suppressed anger, a deeply resentful indignation, an unwillingness to take personal responsibility, while attributing blame onto others.

- *Gluttony* is excessively eating and drinking more than the body needs.

- *Envy* wants what others have.

- *Sloth* is a habitual disinclination to exertion, i.e. laziness.

A working awareness of the seven deadly sins creates a framework for the spiritual journey, a focus of inner work. They provide a structure for working with people when discerning their distractions and issues.

It is also worth exploring the seven virtues as, like all things, taken to extremes they become unhealthy obstacles to authenticity.

- Faith is trust in the belief in an ideal. It requires an ability to discern between the voice for the Holy Spirit and the voice of the ego.

- Hope is taking a positive future view, but not to the detriment of sanity and self care.

- Charity is concern for, and active helping of, others, but again not at the expense of self as it could lead to martyrdom.

- Fortitude is never giving up. It requires wisdom to ensure it does not become an end in its own right.

- Justice is being fair and equitable with others. Be wary of a lack of decision making.

- Prudence is care of and moderation with money, not to be taken to extremes in miserliness.

- Temperance is moderation of consumption and abstinence (which could lead to a form of anorexia if taken to its limits).

Self-rejection

Self-rejection underlies illness. In telling ourselves we are no good, that we are failures, that we can't be trusted, etc., we are reinforcing the lack of self-worth that is the result of a perceived separation from God.

How many times have we said or heard a loved one put off an event, a job, a relationship based on their lack of self-worth? Every day millions of people play small, rejecting their true nature. Who needs others to reject us as we do it so subtly and well ourselves?

How many times have you backed away from some relationship or opportunity because you want to change something about yourself first? Even when we talk ourselves into applying for the best jobs, saying yes to dates with the `hot` people, it may only be a matter of time until our self-worth sabotages it, pushing us back to where we think we really should be. Any conditions or limitations we place on our self are indicative of our worth. Each and every one is a travesty against God as we are saying we know better how much of a loser we are! And if, indeed, we are made in the likeness of the Divine, what does that say about our belief in the Divine?

Worse still, how many people have confirmed our lack of worth by urging us to go for exams, take jobs, lose weight, etc, as *we are not enough as we are now*! And how many people have we encouraged in their lack of worth by agreeing that they need be anything other than who they are right now? It is a fine line indeed, accepting another exactly as they are whilst maintaining that vision of the inner perfection no matter what they chose to believe.

This is the role the Mystic-Healer offers, the gift of holding the vision of the others inner perfection, whilst also being able to meet them where they are now in non-judgmental acceptance.

The healing journey is from self-rejection to self-acceptance. Stepping away from self-denigration of any kind opens us to the inner wonders of who we really are.

It has been said that the light in a person brings us one of two things, either a desire to be like them and open to all the gifts they offer, or jealousy as we see they are where we, on some level, want to be.

Fears
Ego is birthed in the world of fear. "There is nothing to fear but fear itself," Franklin D Roosevelt encouraged the American people in an inaugural address. Fears are linked intimately with our self-worth. As previously discussed, the fear of stepping up to who and what we are, being `seen`, and living fully (the exact state that describes "health") limits our growth and freedom.

Until we have faced our fears we cannot be whole, free, and at peace. Fear is a portal through which we must go before we can be truly healed and healthy, fully ourselves.

The questions, "what would you do if you were healthy?", and "what is stopping you from doing this?", locate the fears which are at the core of holding you back from healing.

Illness is one of the catalysts for change. Confronting mortality is a dynamic experience allowing change to occur naturally.

In this, the 'communication age", the number of people living alone is at record levels. Is this isolation an opportunity to connect with the Divine within? Is this a chance to have the ultimate relationship, with oneself and the indwelling God? Can we really live interdependently with another if we have not yet learned to be at peace with ourselves?

Fear can indicate an unwillingness to surrender to a Higher Power. It is the ego asserting its supremacy. Anything other than love is fear. Even a small amount of fear indicates an unwillingness to surrender, in the same way that you can't be a little bit pregnant.

Fear can impose tunnel vision on our lives and in turn, direct our behavior. Bring to mind a time of fear, what were the limitations that those fears imposed on you in that situation?

Self-punishment is often the after-effect of fear. Most of us punish ourselves when we try and fail to step into who we really are. The ways we do this are varied. Self-punishment manifests as attacks on our bodies through diet, alcohol, drugs, exercise, sex and stress. More subtle ways are denying ourselves experiences, culture, quiet reflection, relationships, times of rest, even fun! It is likely that a court of human rights would not judge us as harshly as our ego does.

Distractions
As we are exploring the role of sickness, it is worth spending a little time looking at the role of distractions. There always have been and always will be ample distractions that can be chosen instead of the healing journey. For example, overwork,

relationship drama, TV, FaceBook and drugs (both legal and illegal), the list goes on.

Each time something emerges that might require us to delve within and perhaps up our game, we can distract in whatever way is our chosen method, soothing, palliating and avoiding opportunities for growth. Identifying a clients modes of avoidance is very useful for seeing where they are out of touch with their core truth.

I had a very obese client many years ago who revealed very little about himself that was useful during the consult. I asked him to come back the following day at the end of the day and to not eat between now and then. He came back and was a very different person, having been unable to soothe the inner distress with food, his true self began to emerge allowing us to meet and work together.

When we can spot the manner in which a person chooses to distract, we can ask them to return having avoided this method of distraction for a period of time prior to the session. In the state of discomfort, they reveal their uncompensated self. We are one step closer to the truth of who they really are.
Consider your own methods of distraction. Confronting them is a significant step on the spiritual journey, bringing you closer to recognizing yourself as everyman.
Mystic–Healers have identified their core distractions, the default behaviors they retreat to and hide in. Only from that degree of self awareness can we see this in another. It does not mean we do not have them. Just that we are aware of them!

Isolation
An emerging epidemic in the western world in the 21st century is that of a deep seated sense of isolation. Mother Teresa spoke last century of "Being unwanted, unloved, uncared for, forgotten by everybody, I think that is a much greater hunger, a much greater poverty than the person who has nothing to eat." Mother Teresa sees the physical poverty of the body in the East,

yet comments that the poverty of the spirit and soul in the West is far more painful.

Isolation is different from loneliness. Isolation requires a geographical distance, a physical disconnect. It is regarded as a serious method of punishing people, hence children send people to `Coventry` when no one is supposed to speak to them, much like a `Time out`, and the penal system uses isolation as ultimate punishment. Loneliness comes more from a disconnect in relationships which explains why so many people feel lonely in a crowd or even in their own family. Many people are now very mobile, keen to move to `better` themselves, breaking families apart and leaving it surprisingly easy to find oneself living alone.

Hospitals have observed that patients undergoing operations have a far greater survival rate when there is someone waiting for them. Our journey is toward reunion, and in this material plane we achieve this through relationships with others. Loneliness is distinct from solitude. Solitude derives from `sol`, the sun, and soul and refers to being alone with a chance to reflect on spiritual matters. Solitude denotes choice.

Co-dependency
Relationships are not all equal. There are those acquaintances we speak to casually in passing for whom we know a name and little more. There are those we socialize with, and there are those with whom we have an invisible link, maybe through friendship, marriage or blood. Just because they are close relationships does not necessarily mean they are easy relationships. We may be drawn to those who are our opposites, as they hold the gift for mutual balance. The gift of their opposition balances our expression and, together, we can move toward the middle ground and balance each other gaining and releasing the imbalances to find the fulcrum.
Supporting the release of behaviors that have served us in palliating fears requires great love. Without this level of love and consciousness, a co-dependent relationship can result,

where each knows the others buttons to press and manipulate to keep the status quo of fear.

Ideally the initial stages of love release our extremes of being and we step together, into greater health, unity and deeper love. When the glow of initial love and merging wanes, co-dependency can appear. Both partners may become polarized as they push each other to the extremes. It takes a good deal of self-awareness and willingness for the relationship to be healthy, in which the couple releases being intertwined, and stands side by side with a shared vision.

Often one party does something that the other does not forgive, yet does not mention. There is a subtle shift, a tiny step back from the loved one, in case they might be hurt again. If the person does not speak up and projects his hurt onto the other, over time it hardens into resentment, separating and dividing the couple incrementally, pushing them to their polar extremes and trapping them in a cycle.

In co-dependent relationships there is some fear being palliated. They tend to remain in this relationship until a greater fear emerges for one of them. In the case of domestic violence, it is often only when there is fear of possible death to self, or injury to loved ones or children, that the impetus to leave will outweigh previously held fears.

Resentment

Resentment is the accumulation of all conscious and subconscious grievances ever felt. It is one of the obstacles to cure that Mystic Healers seek to assist the client in releasing in order for a deep healing to take place.

Resentments compound and reduce the Divine flow that comes through us. The ego catches each offense, each tiny word spoken, each action that it can distort into an attack and stores them up creating an armory of ` I am right-ness`. Once we enter the `I am right`, it tends to result in the `you are wrong` position. With the ego unchecked, the inner pot of righteous indignation, bubbles to overflowing. What better way to express this than by throwing it at another,"They did it!"

The Course in Miracles says 'you can be right or happy". Lonely, isolated and right, or loved, united and happy! Accepting the way things are and releasing the need for them to be different, joy may be gained. Insisting on the need for things to be different no matter how much pain the thoughts give, results in torture. It can only be insanity to choose to be right in ego terms, and then to experience 'rightness' in bitter resentful thoughts and feelings. It makes it easy to see how some traditions externalize the ego in the devil, evil or sin. Who would want to take responsibility for the thoughts and feelings we have? No-one sane would *choose* to feel that way!

Fear underpins the ego's desire to collect all perceived insults and attacks, to store them up and nurture them. Resentments, painful negative feelings, lack of self-worth and self-esteem, anxiety and fear all originate from the ego. Compare this to freedom, happiness, ease of living, union, joy and the deep peace that comes from living on the spiritual path. It is, as the hip say, a total 'no-brainer'!

Judgment

Judgment is a vital part of life, if we don't recognise, i.e. judge, a fire to be hot we risk burning ourselves. This is a valid and sensible use of judgment. However, judgment can also come from the ego, and, at times, be the weapon we defend with. Judgments come from the inner places that we deny, dislike or fear. In a state of full ego, we regard ourselves as perfect and will deny or suppress any aspect of ourselves that does not tie in with the image we have chosen. These internal areas find their expression in our judgments. Projection separates us from others. We become tied into our projections making us servant to the judgment the other embodies for us. Judging others makes us their prisoner. Judgments of others keep us in fear as we remain dependent on being right with these judgments. Conversely, our judgments actively tie us to what we deny or dislike within. The other person is a gift, a mirror reflecting our shadows right back to us.

Sometimes, it is not what we see in others that we are fighting, but the opposite. For example; if we perceive another as arrogant, it might be that we are not manifesting our confidence, but living in false humility, the opposite of arrogance, the same trajectory, but expressing the polar opposite. Until we can see ourselves in the other we are unable to perceive a world of peace since we are chained by the need to feel `right`.

Ironically, our willingness to go within and see who we really are requires us to suspend judgment. If not, many would take one look within and recoil in horror at the truth of how they have lived thus far. Seeing the times of thinking, speaking or acting from fear creates revulsion with self. The spiritual journey advocates compassion as a lens for the opening of self-awareness. Add forgiveness, and we have a powerful tool supporting our inner journey, allowing us to release the image of ourselves that no longer serves.

The saying `physician heal thyself` could be adapted to `physician know thyself`. In knowing ourselves, we are more easily able to release judgments of others. In practice, releasing judgments and allowing a deep connection with the other transforms a session into a mutually beneficial healing opportunity. Just as breathing and digestion are two physical transformations, these encounters offer the chance to transmute our lives from the lead of fear into the gold of love.

No matter what happens to us, it is how we perceive it that defines us. The meaning we give can lead us into hell or fill us with peace. The choice is ours. There is no ultimate good or bad, right or wrong, there is only a choice whether to judge or not; what criterion to apply is ours and as such defines our experience of life.

Guilt

Guilt comes when we realize we have not thought, spoken or acted from love. It highlights areas in which we could rethink our behavior. When we choose to learn from it, it is short lived, and is resolved positively. If we choose not to learn from it, we tend to fail completely through self sabotage, . We often continue the beating repeatedly. What we choose to do with guilt determines whether it is a tool for growth or for suppression.

Failures gives credence to the ego's bedtime story " you are not worthy", "you are not good enough". Guilt grows as we repeat and compound our failures. We may have different ways of expressing this, but we each experience this. It can be corrosive over time. Holding onto guilt and withholding forgiveness locks oneself away in a prison with no windows, light or key. In hopelessness, there is madness.

As mentioned, guilt may be a warning light that a change is needed. An overly energetic religious belief system may hammer people with worthlessness and guilt, or they may not know what to believe in or how to discern it. The spiritual journey brings up many questions, are we worthless or humble? Are we co-creators with God or deluded egomaniacs?

Guilt can be experienced as a gift if we release it and move on with more self-awareness. If the guilt isn't acted on in this way, it becomes inappropriate, an obstacle to cure, blocking the flow of love that is healing. God never judged in the first place, we do that all by ourselves! When self-blame continues, guilt starts to move into pathology. To avoid the guilt, we avoid situations that might have us open to experiencing guilt. Our lives reduce as we start to limit our freedom to avoid the possibility of guilt.

The Gifts of Sickness

The gift of sickness is in it's potential to awaken us to look beyond the external self. The questions we ask determine our future lives, as well as the answers we choose to accept. Without something to give us the wakeup call, we have no reason to look beyond. Illness is perfect in personalizing a manifestation for each individual. It offers each individual the time to retune thinking in a way they are able to 'get it'.

Homesickness

Living in congruence with our core belief creates a peace-filled fearless life. This is our natural state, a place we intuitively know as 'home'. When, for whatever reason, we step out of integrity, our soul cries out. Our soul yearns for home, for a return to a place where harmony and peace dwell.

All aspects of the need for belonging are manifestations of misalignment. The soul will perpetually call us home. Examples might be a shared club, a fashion statement, food choices, or any form of seeking to belong to another. The solution to homesickness is closer than the beating of your heart, wherein the indwelling, permanently present God resides. Hope can be the cruelest of virtues when we foolishly try the same thing again and again, sadly getting the same result each time. Returning home is the unconscious desire; returning is the dynamic that drives our unconscious and sometimes conscious lives. *We are homesick for ourselves*; initially we came from our mother dividing the one into two. Slowly we pull away from this union, only to spend the rest of our lives trying to return into another to find ourselves as we look for another to complete us in order to become a `Oneness` again. How many people have a sense of `wholeness` when they fall in love? A sense of union describes the powerful effect that merging with another has.

Reunion can have a powerful effect on us. The scenes of reunion at airports is a classic example of the depth of emotion that reunion creates. There is, however, a loss that precedes the joy of reunion. The loss is linked to our soul purpose; when we step out of Divine alignment we `lose` a part of ourselves that we seek, this is, in truth, the Holy Grail. When we are younger we externalize the search as we travel the world looking everywhere for this missing piece. We look to others to provide it in relationships. As we get older, the travel and relationships may wear thin, not having held their early promise of being the answer. We may try yet another journey or relationship, or we may finally start to look elsewhere.

Often it takes a crisis before we realize that the search was addressing the wrong questions. Now the questions are reformed, refined and asked again, instigating another journey, this time within.

Transformation
A serious illness, redundancy or job loss, a breakdown in yet another relationship, or the death of a loved one are all potentials for change. The pain these events evoke can either burn us up in resentment, bitterness or denial or become the stimulus for transformation. These events create the crucible for alchemical transformation through physical experience into spiritual growth. The choice is ours. Do we step into victim and blame the external world for all our misfortunes? Or do we take self responsibility and, like the phoenix, rise from the ashes of pain and disaster to be truly reborn deeper into ourselves?

Through reflection, we may find a patterned way of responding to events that has repeated throughout our lives. When a situation finally occurs that our usual coping mechanism cannot deal with, it can become the catalyst for transformation. For one person this might be getting the flu, for another it might be cancer. It matters not how serious the illness or event is, it will be as `loud` as it needs to be to get our attention. This event, in homoeopathic terms, is the aggravation.

After a homoeopathic remedy is given, the presenting state is enhanced in order for the inner self healing mechanism to react. It is as if this enhanced expression of ourselves is a wakeup call, magnifying us so we really see within. It is calling us to account. An example is an underweight person with their clothes telling them what they have denied seeing on the scale. It is themselves in bold font. The realization dawns that they are, indeed, underweight and something needs to be addressed.

The role of sickness, when we see it as the spiritual journey, is to provide a wakeup call, an opportunity to look within to where the truth lies. We get whatever it is that we need in order to be willing to explore within, to open to self awareness.

The process of healing requires us to release the ego to see through the eyes of love and unity. We are like Narcissus, falling in love with his physical reflection and dying as he was unable to leave his own image, when we don't go through transformation in whatever way it presents itself. In this state we are limited to living life through the lens of the ego. A life stuck in perceiving each event as an attack, remaining hell-bound in personal and projected judgment.

Illness offers us the chance to look deeper within, to fall in love with our own soul, the place within where the Divine lives, the place where we are truly home.
The gift of sickness is the wakeup call to the freedom of living with love in a fearless world.

Sickness is a time to stop and reflect, to listen. It is a time to allow the soul to ferment and life's experiences to percolate deeper, enriching our perception and worldview, as it transmutes into wisdom. It could be said that adversity is the hammer that cracks open the shell of the heart, allowing compassion to flow. Without any external challenges we may not grow, change, mature and make fresh new sense of life. The Course in Miracles tells us that it is not up to us what we learn, but whether we choose to learn through joy or pain!

The Sufi mystic Hafiz said:

> *"You can come to God dressed for Dancing*
> *Or*
> *Be carried on a stretcher to God's ward."*

We do have choice; we have to do whatever we have to do, yet we can go gracefully with open arms or fight, struggle and resist like a two year old having a tantrum.

Aging offers the gift of an opportunity to meet challenges and transcend them.
If life is a perpetually revolving circle, then opening to the spiritual journey reshapes this circle into an ever-enlarging spiral affording us a greater view, an enlarged context in which to place each event or challenge.

It is sad that sickness is condemned and judged in the western world when it's real role is dynamic, restorative and transformational. Epiphanies of inner truth accrue incrementally, freeing us from the chains of the ego. Once we realise each truth, and step into the freedom to be who we really are, our health improves on all levels, physically in making healthier choices in lifestyle, and mentally and emotionally as we release the need for judgment and projection. We release the thousands of man made laws to abide by Universal Law.

This process requires courage! Much may need to change for our choices to reflect our new awareness. This is a huge commitment to growth, yet anything less keeps us stuck in a lack of integrity, an incongruence between knowing and behaving which cycles back into an inner disconnect and holds us in our old way of being. Pain can burn us up or it can transform us, the choice is ours. Illness can be the crucible for healing.

The Role of Symptoms
Signs and symptoms, as used here, describe anything mental, emotional or physical that is an indication of a disorder in a person. Signs and symptoms might be as seemingly innocuous as an aversion to hot drinks or it might be a cancer eroding the body. Each sign or symptom offers insight into aspects of the person. They represent flags alerting us to look within and reassess the congruence of our choices thus far. If we don't listen, we may be hit over the head with a baseball bat disguised as a diagnosis. Ouch! At last we stop and explore.

Signs or symptoms appear on the mental and emotional level long before reaching the body. They originate in the person's world view. For example, a person may seek to palliate a feeling of inadequacy. When, after much trying, this palliation fails to soothe, the disturbance deepens. The self healing mechanism kicks in and throws the inner disturbance to the farthest part of our self, namely the body. If suppressed with pills and potions, it is pushed back deeper in the economy, so the original inadequacy starts to fragment into shards of glass bringing feelings of jealousy, a desire for vengeance, etc. Society sometimes reduces the definition of signs and symptoms to include only physical ones, disregarding feelings and perceptions. The western world views symptoms as problems to be fixed, sorted, or removed, yet what if the opposite is true?

Signs and symptoms could be described as the door knocker of conscious awareness trying to surface. They are an invitation to stop and look deeper, offering us a time for reflection and reevaluation. Signs and symptoms are essential communications from God, they hold a promise of healing when they are recognised for their value. It could be asked whether the sign or symptom has us, or do we have it? Does it come from us or manifest through us?

The role of the Mystic Healer is to see the signs and symptoms as the communication of the Vital Force which is the representative of the soul. A sign or symptom is a way into a person's story, it creates an opening for vulnerability. Pain debilitates, dissolving defences, offering a portal to the soul, a route home. Signs and symptoms indicate duality as in their very existence they denote imbalance.

Embrace the pain as part of life's experience, it opens up compassion. This experience is halted by modern medicine when it removes the symptom, restricting us to a limited life, removing the gift of potential growth and delaying our journey into personal freedom and peace. After many repetitions of palliation, the mode of expression will likely deepen to a more serious, potentially life threatening disease or organ system. It generally progresses until it reaches the level where we take notice, where we are broken. It is in the brokenness of life that we meet God.

We are self healing organisms – that is inherent anima-animus, the Vital Force is continually trying to recalibrate us back to Divine Alignment – all signs and symptoms are signposts of the soul, look and listen.

Susceptibility is the portal to Divine alignment, the place through which we realign with our sacred mission. It is the greatest, most exciting journey of all, to learn the truth of who you really are.

It is our deepest vulnerability. It is human nature to protect it by surrounding it with fear. All the heroic tales of mythology and film are analogies of going to the portal within. In the adventure that is our life, entering this place of vulnerability requires us to confront the protective fears in order to grow.

Vulnerability creates the crisis in each one of us in the precise way in which we are in need of healing. The protective fears lead to illness as the Vital Force constantly tries to move us toward and through our susceptibility. It is only when we have touched susceptibility that we can move through with open tender heart and enter union with others in deep humility knowing we are truly One.

The aim of the Mystic-Healer is to hold the space for the other to feel safe enough to move toward and through their vulnerability, secure in the compassionate strength of the Mystic-Healer.

"A mystic is one who has moved from mere belief systems or belonging systems to actual inner experience"
Father Richard Rohr

Healing – *The Journey*

Again, the goal of health is reunion with the indwelling Divine, your God, moving beyond the duality of the material world and returning to the non-dual state of Oneness. In this oneness, boundaries are lost and total communion with all of nature, with all people and with God is embraced.

Healing is a verb, denoting energy, movement, a dynamic impulse toward health. Health may be experienced as inner peace of heart and mind, a body not at war with itself, an ego working in tandem with our Higher good. Health is a return to the truth of who we are, healing is the journey. Sickness offers a time where we can chose to forgo the external search for meaning and, by accepting the gifts of the sickness and its impetus into questioning, turn the journey around, head homewards within, where our Higher self has been waiting all this time. Inner health is constant, healing is the journey, our only choice is when we decide to take the journey home to true health.

The healing journey takes but a nanosecond to start, it is just a choice. This choice is frequently made under some form of duress the ego cannot contain, when the ego cannot cope with familiar choices. This willingness to learn the truth of who we really are lights the touch paper, from which there is no going back. The saying ignorance is bliss is quite profound, once we have seen a different way of being, even just a mere glimpse of the potential of transformation, there is no going back. We may fight and resist, but it is just a matter of time until the ego buckles as it cannot sustain the illusions any longer. It can happen in a moment, or it can take years, again the only choice we have is willingness. The willingness is to step out of fear and embrace love.

The healing journey represents the release of ego and the transformation this offers, being courageous enough to dive into the fear so it can be burned up in the crucible of consciousness.

This journey introduces us to a whole new way of being, a landscape we have never seen before, with a whole new set of guides. It opens us up to a world beyond anything we can understand in this material world. In truth, the concepts and reality of this inner mystical world are beyond our comprehension, words cannot begin to represent it. Hence the mystics of all traditions struggled to find words, using analogies and parables to make the incomprehensible as accessible as possible.

The Homoeopathic understanding of health involves the Law of Cure which regards the soul as the deepest point we can connect to, around this lies our mental and then emotional fields. The inner self-healing mechanism will always seek the least life threatening way to vent the internal disorder. The breakdown of the person's ability to stay in denial and fear will manifest on the surface, moving deeper when the initial mode of expression is palliated into suppression. At this point the inner disturbance will seek the next 'safe' mode of expression. The denial offered by palliation and suppression push the person deeper into fear and ultimately a breakdown when 'they', the ego, can no longer cope. At this point the real, heartfelt deep healing can begin.

The Holy Trinity is thought, word and deed, ultimate alignment of energy and matter, God and humanity. Herein lies health, our goal with healing as the vehicle for the journey home.
Ken Wilbur writes of the unique experience mystics have that can be summed up in 'Deus factus sum – I have become God. While this may be the ultimate goal of life itself, experiencing it here, on earth is the goal of the Mystic-Healer.

Healing is about joining, reconnecting 're-union', thus implying a previous connected state. In Buddhism, the image is that of the ocean with each one of us discreet like the seemingly individual waves, yet when the time comes, the wave is subsumed back into the sea, returning to where it emerged, to itself.
This is classically seen in lovers as they meet, merge and become 'lost' in each other. It is this loss of egoic separate self

that is behind the yearning for love that Hollywood so well exploits. Whereas, in truth, the love we yearn for externally is really the search for the God within, our sense of home where we belong. Healing is the verb in our quest for Oneness where we merge with others, with nature, with God.

When we are `in love`, we are happy, we smile, our defenses are down and we are much more likely to merge with others. Interestingly, we are at our best during this tender time of deep vulnerability. Nothing external has changed, yet love transforms how we perceive the world. Love makes things brighter, bigger, lovelier, more optimistic. Love can be addictive as it affords us a touch of heaven, a tantalizing reminder of what it is like to live with love, to be surrounded and filled with love. If the ego kicks in, however, and the inner voice perceives our loved one has `done us wrong` in some way or another, it starts to whisper `what about me?`

It is a conundrum to yearn to merge with all whilst inhabiting a separate human form. Is promiscuity a vain and desperate attempt to do just this? Is it an attempt to annihilate a sense of isolation? Any such strategy not built on the foundation of love is destined to repeat endlessly until we realise that this way of being creates more problems than it could possibly offset. Without a commitment to love and respect, very often we arrive at the point of questioning provoked by some occasion that the ego cannot handle, such as the guise of illness.

Relationships offer the gift of belonging. Belonging is admitting who you are. It is a place to share with others who express their humanity in a similar way. It offers shared language, shared emotions, and shared interests that connect us. From this place of connection we expand with another and our energies blend, each giving and receiving from the other. This is the eternal dance of Divine unity playing out over the ages. This dance takes us from the bleak and bitter desolation of loneliness to the technicolour joys and deep peace of union that are the gifts of the Divine, the Holy Spirit. This can happen in relationship with another human, ourselves, an animal, a practice, nature itself, etc.

The healing journey is the spiritual journey, it is our voyage into giving and being able to receive unconditional love. Home is where we are vessels allowing this to flow through us and become us.

Divine Flow (The Tao)

Flow is vital as it reminds us that we are merely conduits for the Holy Spirit, servants of the dynamic, not the masters. In practice, our role as Mystic-Healers is to do our best, release attachment to outcome, and trust that the person's inner healing mechanism knows what to do.

When we allow the Higher energies of nature full sway without interference, we may come to understand the expression of the Vital Force. Taoism describes this energy flow poetically, and for those in the health related professions, Taoist Haven Trevino has written an incomparable reference book entitled "The Tao of Healing" which is pure poetry on this subject.

The Tao is the journey home, it is the verb of life itself. Two hundred years ago Samuel Hahnemann said "The physician's role is to "to *restore* the sick to health… rapid, gentle and permanent *restoration* of health…in the shortest, most reliable, and most harmless way" which is by going with the flow of the energy seen in the person's expression of self as manifest in symptoms.

Our role is to identify the natural flow, not to limit or restrain it in any way. Recognizing it in ourselves allows us to recognize it more easily in others. When we are open and self-aware, we can more easily see where and how we have been the limitation in whatever healing modality we offer. No matter how committed we are to expanding self awareness, it is an on-going life time of discovering more and more subtle expressions of egoic limitation. Like a good man who realized one night when saying his final prayers, thanking God for the day, how he had been kind, considerate, patient etc., only to realize at the very end of the prayers, that pride has sneaked in there while he was unaware!

Constant vigilance is required to be able to discern the Divine Flow in ourselves or others. Willingness to explore all the boulders and rocks that clutter up and block the free, deep and powerful flow is what makes healing possible.

Detachment

Genuine deep healing requires detachment from the ego, i.e., there would be no expectations of the person, the healer, the therapeutic tool or the outcome of the other's healing process. Attachment creates a lens through which we observe a distorted version of the world.

Clarity of perception is clouded by meanings we ascribe. They prevent us from seeing, hearing and being fully present to what is happening right here and right now.
Releasing meaning is a step toward freedom. We cannot release the past while we are attached to it, the very notion is an oxymoron. Is it not these unresolved attachments to earlier events that cloud the present in every way? It is easy to see how life repeats itself as we project the attachments of the past onto the present, and thereby reinforce the distorted perception.

The healing dynamic, the Vital Force, the universe, they are all impersonal as they are detached and from a place of non-duality. Life is impersonal. Events and people can only hurt us if we are attached to them. When we discern the fear that fuels the attachment, we grow through releasing the attachment to fear!

The process of deconstruction is a spiritual experience. It burns away the pain of expectation and inevitable disappointment. Releasing attachments cuts the chains that restrict freedom.

The life events a person is attached to are useful in the therapeutic relationship, they are a route into the core of the person. In each place of pain is the whole of the case, the microcosm seen in the macrocosm, the holographic effect. As we work with others, helping them identify the moments when a deep fear was activated, poked or prodded enough for the innate healing mechanism to respond protectively, we facilitate an opening to consciousness, self awareness, which is the route of healing.

Healing is releasing attachment to the material world in every form, people, lifestyle, jobs, status, possessions, and of course, ego, while focusing wholly on the God within.
When a client tells us that `they have never said this to anyone before`, or `have never thought of it that way before`, it is an indication that healing has begun, there is a shift in consciousness.

Internal validation
The time comes for releasing attachment to the outer validation, from needing other people to define who we think we are by their opinions of us. Considering they are as attached and fearful as we are, whom do we actually believe? Do we believe their thoughts of us, or their recognition of themselves as reflected by us? It is utterly insane to believe another's opinions without question. Yes, they might have an observation that might serve us, but to stay `sane` we need to be able to discriminate.

Healing starts when we can hear the small still voice within and are able to heed its guidance. Discernment between the inner voices is a constant challenge. Asking each voice if it is unifying or fear based is a powerful criteria to apply.

This inner self-healing mechanism, the Vital Force, has been likened to the vice regent to the soul. The soul has a consciousness of Divinity and is our umbilical cord to God. In the physical world it connects the body and God, it is the hotline to God. As all symptoms and disease come from loss of integrity, symptoms are crackles on the divine link, static on the line that we need to adjust to get a crystal clear connection.

Acceptance

Healing comes through acceptance of self as part of the greater totality, not as a separate entity. If we see illness as external and happening to us, then energy is wasted projecting outwards, fighting a war with the unfindable enemy. The truth is kinder and resides within.

In the 21st century, we are seeing a rise in autoimmune diseases, where the body is literally rejecting itself. Might this be an expression of the degree of externalization inherent in the western world view? Or might it be the ultimate result of regarding any illness as external and thus fighting it? This externalization is a war with the outer, autoimmunity is an internal war. Where can the ego go from here?

Recently a friend wrote a piece for an auto-immune website about wholism and was astonished at the number and intensity of vitriolic rejections his article provoked. The group behaved like the disease, attacking its own membership.

In all this warfare there is the desire to win, not lose, to be right. In both cases it is a polar duality that is behind the war. Every judgment, good or bad, is a projection and expression of the internal war.

Releasing judgment of others, taking responsibility for looking within and owning all that is there brings with it a quiet deep acceptance of others exactly as they are. In Christianity this is `loving the sinner not the sin`, referring to the ability to love the perfect person deep within the other, not needing to judge their latest expression of who they think they are!

When we are able to see and hold the vision for the other's inner beauty when they fail to see or accept themselves in this way, we offer a gift as Mystic-Healers, that of holy vision.

Love

Love is the dynamic in which unifying occurs. When we release expectation and judgment, when we remove the barriers that our defenses put into place, we can be fully present to be there wholly to another. In this wholeness is love and anything is possible. It isn't possible to be a little bit loving. Like with pregnancy, you either are or you are not pregnant. We either love or we do not love, in other words we are living in fear. There are no halfway stages. Love heals all wounds. From a mother kissing a bump or bruise better, to a hand reaching out to one in utter despair, saying, you are not alone. Together anything is possible.

Christ consciousness

Christ is a worldwide symbol for healing. From the depth of his authentic humanity he rose to embody the divine within. This is the heart of the mystic healer. All mystics throughout time have met the father /mother (duality, yin/yang, Divine Masculine/Feminine) within and in so doing reunited man and God closing the gap of separation, transcending common humanity for humanity as God. This is the role to which the Mystic-Healer aspires.

There are many examples of healing work in which disabled and infirm were made whole again. This is achieved through the wholehearted ability to perceive the other as sinless, without ailment of disease in any form, to be able to see the God within them where we are all One. From that depth of vision the other was met at the place where God and Mankind merge. Interestingly enough it is from the ability to accept self as 100% human that Divinity arises.

This level of self-acceptance links the individual soul to the soul of the world, this makes the ordinary transform into the extra-ordinary. This is the world of miracles.

Tools for Healing

Mystery, acceptance
There is a lot to be said for the science of today. We can see and understand things in a way our ancestors could never believe. However, this knowledge can stop us from trusting what we experience, but cannot `prove`. We may limit our lives by needing to understand fully and completely before making decisions. Ego will resist all attempts to take the source of personal power from the intellect to the intuition. Using both intellect and intuition wisely is the ideal.

Our belief in the ego as real limits our healing to the ways in which we `think` it can happen. Rather than allow healing to occur, many people unconsciously place their faith in a familiar medicine system and restrict the path to health.

Why not ask for healing and allow it to occur in whatever way is best for us? Simple trust opens potential to its fullest.

Surrender
Surrendering our relationship with fear allows us to dive more fully into love. The ego has to surrender the desire to play god for Unity in order for healing to occur.

The Sufis speak of death before dying, the Buddhists talk of knowing death before one can fully live. The tribes of many nations have rites of passage where mortality and fear are faced in order to facilitate growth. These references to `death` are the ego death. Death of the ego is a release from attachment to fear, however it is expressed or palliated. It is surrender to a dynamic infinite universe.

Fear is the area we most avoid, and the place we most need to visit for healing to occur. In homeopathic terms, the aggravation represents the point momentarily prior to the ego's disintegration.

We are terrified of a loss of `self`. If `we` do not exist, then what is there? Our minds and hearts are challenged to envisage the enormity that genuine surrender and consequent union offer. To be as a grain of sand in the universe of stars and galaxies is frightening and lonely, the spiritual journey is the path from this fear to becoming the sand, the stars and the universe.

Our journey into healing goes through the heart of true love, not the center of egoic love (where all suffering comes from). It is through experiential healing, entering into the hurt of the heart, that the potential to move through it arises. This cannot happen if we are palliating, distracting or suppressing. In opening to the crashing waves of emotional pain as our ego surrenders, our soul swoops in to hold us in calm waters, to bring us safely to the shores of the universe.

Living a mystical life requires surrendering the illusion of control, that we can arrange our lives as we want! It takes willingness to do what it takes to re-align with the Divine. What matters most to you is what you have to release, as it represents your greatest attachment. These attachments anchor us in the unreal world of materialism.

So what would you give up to be healed? And, of course, what are you not prepared to give up? How much does healing and inner peace mean to you?

Life is impermanence and change. Remaining in thrall to a material thing or a concept mimics the denial and delusion of King Canute! Once we really understand the tidal flow of every part of life, it becomes so much easier to release attachment to things being a certain way, or to control. As said before it is not what life throws at us, but how we deal with it that defines us. Not only does it define us, but it brings into vivid relief where we need to shine our inner light and open to enhanced awareness.

One can also go too far and become out of balance with welcoming change. It can be an addiction in its own right depending upon the intention behind each action. It is the intention behind the action that is important; a man wielding a scalpel with a body in front of himm might be a surgeon or a murderer.

The willingness to release material attachment is proportional to the depth of commitment to the goal of re-union. Isn't is quite something to know oneself so well that all attachments can be seen, and yet a person could still be unable to let go of them? Maybe the only prayer we need is willingness. `Beloved, help me release what does not serve, Amen.`
What would you die for, what are you willing to live for?

Surrender is visible not so much in living in poverty of possessions, but in humility, being receptive to all, being non-judgmental, and appreciating all that is. Surrender is visible in releasing the need to understand everything.

Divine connection is experienced when we surrender the need to explain. Mystics of old often made no mention of their mystical encounters as they defy mere speech. They treated these moments with deep respect. The true awe with which these experiences are received would be reduced and limited in trying to describe them.

Alchemical transformation

The healing journey is alchemical in nature.

The alchemical catalyst at each stage creates the fire required to burn off the egoic attachment to each world view. It may be a belief in possessions that is transformed by the fire of job loss igniting a fear of poverty which catalyses questions on the meaning for life which can lead into a deeper world view. Or it may be a sole focus on the appearance of the body, being destroyed through illness, leading the person within. This is when the inner world becomes more real and stable. The healing is in the movement, the journey of awakening that is experienced when the need for external validation dissolves into and integrates the inner world and God-self-belief. Each release, each change of perception, incrementally accrues and creates the ever expanding spiral of increased awareness that is the healing journey of life.

Fear is the alchemic agent. Courage, the fire of the soul, has to burn us in order to refine us. Fear is the protector of the inner vulnerable places and the guardian of the ego, ensuring the person never enters the fires of change. The vulnerable places are the portals to the Divine. The ego fights our attempts to enter the surrendered place of peace that exists on the other side of the fears of ego.

How might life look if you could dissolve the fears? If you could face and embrace them, what would be on the other side? If all the palliations put in defensive place were not required and could be released, life would expand exponentially allowing you to live life to the fullest, to reach your full potential.

Transformation happens through continued willingness to look within, to embrace each step deeper into love as this changes how we perceive the world. It is from this awareness that we can see each option as it arises and chose which perception to view it from. This frees us up to retain personal power and not be subsumed by fear. This is wisdom.

The process of awakening begins with us unaware of the inner journey, so in a place of being unconsciously incompetent. Once we start to explore the inner life we step into conscious incompetence and as we use this awareness to grow, we move into a place of conscious competence which, with time and practice becomes the norm, a place of unconscious competence. However this last step is never recognised as it occurs only being appreciated in retrospection.

If we relinquish our reliance on who we once thought we were, we reach deeper within to the truth. This relinquishment of our idea of self is what the Sufi's mean when they speak of `dying before death`.

Thomas Merton, a Cistercian monk from the twentieth century speaks of false self and True self. We have to die to the false self in order to release the True self. It is the alchemical process. Man continually yearns for and seeks through the known external universe for this process, yet it is within us the whole time. There is no greater or deeper learning than through experience.

Healing is the journey from the disintegration of health to the re-turning to life. From ceasing to believe in the story we have woven for ourselves and starting to trust our relationship with the Divine spark within. It happens when we change our mind about which inner voice to believe. It is as simple as that!

Awareness
For people involved in any way with the healing dynamic, the process of increasing the capacity for awareness is essential.

Awareness is a necessary prerequisite to authenticity. Stepping out of egocentricity where other countries, people, circumstances and situations are concerned, and into an awareness of other people and their conditions of living is an important step in connecting with other as self. Whilst this is admirable, our degree of self-awareness determines how open to the rest of the world we can be. As much as we are in the world, the world is in us!

Responsibility is a side effect of developing self-awareness. Living in integrity demands that we live to our greatest degree of self-awareness. In integrity, it would be impossible to have an affair as it would be impossible not to consider the effects on the betrayed parties and feel their pain. It would be impossible to step into self-awareness and then steal from the boss. The internal discordance would lead to illness. A betrayal of the gnosis of a more conscious life betrays our inner divinity. It does not compute. I recall a very dear friend saying with great sadness, how ignorance really was bliss as she was rejecting a course of hedonistic action that would once have brought her `fun`!

Each stage of expansion in self awareness involves recognition, followed by understanding and finally absorbing and embodying the new and enlarged worldview. At the stage of understanding, we see the newer stage of awareness we wish to embrace, but have yet to let go of our previous way of being. In recognising one stage and releasing the other, taking the understanding and experience of the previous stage with us, we integrate in a distillation of self.

Since any change in one affects all the satellites that come into their orbit, our growth in awareness can be a challenge for our loved ones and friends. They may well try, albeit unconsciously, to keep us where it suits them, thus putting pressure on us to remain the same. This state of tension, if not resolved, can lead to illness as the dynamic drive to Unity propels us forward. The result is often fractured relationships as the parties play out their changed dynamics and need to pull apart to reform in a different, more expanded manner. It can be a painful, angst-ridden time of blame and projection, of a sense of rejection and loss. With awareness, it can be smoother, more graceful and ultimately, an opportunity for both to grow together.

Self knowledge

Self awareness can be scary. Looking within, we discover things we dislike about ourselves, judgments, which we invariably project onto others. Healthy self –awareness requires self-acceptance. Releasing the need to judge transforms self-aware-ness into the path of `gnosis`, the divine knowledge of who we are as part of the Source of All.

On a day to day basis, self-awareness and self-acceptance manifest in self-esteem. How much do we esteem the self? Our parent's words and actions validate our existence. Our sense of worth in childhood comes from this validation. How much are we worth? How have we experienced ourselves as children? How are we seen through the eyes of our parents? This viewpoint creates the internal voice that limits us. Ideally we are loved, valued and filled with worth. When we are, we step fully into self-validation. For many people it is not quite this ideal. We are as worthy as our parents envision us to be which depends on their own self-esteem. It is here that we see the `sins of the fathers` visited on the offspring.

A healthy self image comes from positive, life affirming experiences.

We see the world based on how we perceive ourselves within it. If we have low self-esteem, we see the world and everyone in it in those terms and we underplay our role. Each of us has a role to play in the transformation of humanity, we all need to be `fully` ourselves, with healthy self-esteem in order for `heaven` to appear on earth.

Yet even if we succeed in an area, self esteem is still dependent on our experience of it. We may be a famous film star/astronaut/ etc, yet still not *experience* ourselves as such.

Accepting the self is a huge step as it often directly opposes what we have been taught. It can be a `two steps forward, one step back` journey for a while, like waking up after a long sleep and needing a wee while for the eyes to adjust to see clearly. It can feel disrespectful to our parents, and other loved ones, who may take it as a rejection of them and their ways. We cannot escape the truth. We can try to deny it, but we can never escape it. Once we surrender to it, the relief of authenticity floods over us like a tsunami of peace, smoothing the journey to the centre of the Oneness of humanity forward.

Discerning our own criteria and releasing attachment to previously imposed values is a step toward authenticity. When we release fear and open to love, we move from external validation to internal validation. When we let go of self-rejection and embrace self-acceptance, we move our vision from other's opinions to that of God.

When the I of ego is released, the true merging and being part of the greater totality of the Divine is possible . True deep self-esteem is that inner gnosis that we are part of this greater totality, this is so profound that it takes a sense of self-esteem to be able to dissolve into it.

Beauty
Beauty is a portal to God, an experience of awe and wonder at something so beyond mere mortal endeavor that the separate self dissolves away. Beauty can transport us, taking us out of intellect into a place that is limitless, ethereal and real, allowing our souls to fully engage. This can be true of art, nature, or music; beauty in any guise will do. There are no words capable of reflecting the language of the soul.

Dissolving the ego induces a silent awe of wonder at the enormity of what lies beyond it, a vision of what can be, of what heaven might look like. It can be too much for many people. Beauty can be mind blowing and scary as it takes us beyond our comfort zone, into the greater limitless potential of God.

Forgiveness
Before we explore forgiveness and its alchemical power, it is important to look at why forgiveness is so important. As we have already discussed, the goal of the ego is to always be right, special and separate. Consequently, any aspects of ourselves we are unwilling to own, which might deflect from our `perfection`, may be denied by projection onto others.
The behavior of others, which is a reflection of some shadow or hidden aspect of ourselves, rings our bells and pushes us into feeling grief and projecting blame and resentment onto others, keeping grievances alive. We have to keep these feelings alive to stay in the place of `rightness`, or denial. The word

resentment comes from the Latin 'resentire – to feel again'. There is no logic here, except for the ego's need to be right. Why would we want to keep bringing to mind something that causes us to feel pain, betrayal, hurt, grief, and anguish unless the ego wants to punish us? The ego is a very hard taskmaster and is never satisfied. It strives to make us *think* we should be more than the glorious truth of who we really are. The ego has us in bondage to memories, and these memories are distorted through the lens of our own denial. Only when we forgive can we lay the demons of the ego to rest.

The effect of keeping alive past grievances is that we stay there frozen in the place of pain, living like hamsters going round on the treadmill, bringing to mind situations in which we felt slighted, wallowing in self pity and projection, then fueling resentment in a vicious cycle of self –torture, with no way out. In this state, growth is held in place and our current decisions and future planning are distorted by the memories constricting our freedom.

Judgment

Judgment is where the ego unleashes its greatest weapons. When we judge others, it tells us more about our own fears than it tells us about the other, we are, unconsciously and unwittingly, seeing in the other an aspect of ourselves that we have denied, suppressed or are totally unaware of. The ego compares with everyone and always manages to find a way to separate.

We can use the ego's judgement as a tool for expanding awareness. Judgment is a potentised version of the mirroring of the Law of Similars. If we so choose, we can start to bring conscious awareness to the judgments that we make and move deeper into self-awareness. This choice represents the deepest aspect of free will. We can 'chose' to be our better selves.

Once we identify this facet of ourselves, we can choose to accept it or to deny it, and behave accordingly. Sometimes we will choose to accept this facet, other times maybe we won't.

Challenges can only be challenges if they tie into fears and will thus be different for each of us and manifest uniquely. The hero's journey is written about in all centuries, cultures, and societies, in myths and legends, from the Holy Grail stories to the Indiana Jones' films.

Behind grievance is judgment. We are glowing love filled beings of light. Our opinion is our ego on steroids!

We always see each other to the level of our own self awareness. This works two ways. Either we see in the other an aspect of ourselves we are in denial over, or we see them reflect back exactly where we are, which we may like or dislike. In both cases, our egos are stirred to react in a negative manner. Resentment and hatred limit our life and freedom. When we are bitter and twisted, we are trapped in an emotional prison. Negative emotions contaminate every facet of our existence and the only person suffering is us. We chose this for ourselves; this is a definition of insanity!

Forgiveness
Each judgment we make is an opportunity for forgiveness. When we choose to release anger, judgment and resentment, we move toward Divine alignment.

Passivity and waiting for the desire to forgive is the ego fooling you yet again. No amount of waiting makes the memories fade and forgiveness wash over you. When we are able to release the other from the tentacles of blame with which we have bound them, we are released.

Caroline Myss describes healing as a release achieved when we give up the need to punish those who have hurt or humiliated us. The desire for vengeance is a dark truth, though we rarely admit it, and is perhaps the greatest reason that we find forgiveness difficult. The greater the fear of what lies within, the greater the desire to project and externalize, hence greater, more punitive forms of vengeance are enacted. Yet, only through forgiveness is the broken heart healed.

Forgiveness is an exciting expression of free will, _we can_ chose to forgive. It can be as simple as that. Forgiveness breaks the chains and patterns that limit individuals, families, communities and countries.

Forgiveness is not limited to a physical experience or situation, it is the gift of Grace blessing an open, willing heart. It represents a shift in consciousness, surrender from the fear of humiliation and shame, into a trust in the Divine flow and the quantum entanglement of all. Each forgiveness impacts the world, severing the invisible ties to `rightness`, judgment and blame. It frees us from the past to live fully present in the now.

Healing is possible with a release of resentment and `rightness`. Pride and forgiveness are polar opposites. In the therapeutic situation, it is helpful to discover the fear beneath the pride. The Course in Miracles says that "anything that is not love is a cry for love". Anything that is not loving and unifying is from the ego and a call for love. This includes love for ourselves exactly as we are.

Forgiveness is the greatest healer revealing the Divine in our wounds of judgment. What happens to us in life just happens! That is it, there is nothing more. When we add in the distorted lenses of fear, expectation, entitlement, and desire, ego, pain and hurt can creep in. Pain comes directly from our attachments to our expectations, to how **we _think_** things should be.

Stages of Forgiveness

Ego/ego - We are RIGHT and refuse to forgive. This is prior to the first stage of forgiveness as it comes from complete personal denial and the subsequent projection onto another.

Ego – We are prepared to have the high ground and `forgive` - a state of false innocence.
This is the first real stage as we have some awareness that forgiveness` is a good thing even if that awareness is linked to something we have learned intellectually rather than a heartfelt decision. From here the desire to forgive grows, even if, at this stage, it is based on the knowledge that it is better for us to forgive than for anyone we might need to forgive. It is still all about what we can get out of it. The payoff is for us.

Heart We want to forgive but just don't know how. When we can't forgive, we can still open to love, allow it to fill and surround us. Grace is the catalyst for forgiveness. Here we are stepping into a genuine desire to forgive, a willingness to really forgive, coupled with a genuine confusion as to how to go about it.

Heart/Soul We pray to forgive and do so, until reminded of the incident and then find a need to pray all over again. This stage is when we have the understanding that prayer is the answer. Physical gestures may help the transition into forgiveness, but it is at the level of prayer that dynamic transformation takes place. The willingness to turn and return to prayer, asking for divine help, ensures that the problem is held in the highest realm where all prayers are answered. As Einstein famously said, "no problem can be solved at the level at which it originated". Surrendering the `righteous ego` and placing it in the hands of the Divine transforms forgiveness into a mystical directive.

Soul – We forget as there is nothing to forgive... we are all One and see beneath actions to the soul beneath.

How to forgive

This is the hard part. When full of resentment and hurt, how do we start to forgive the offender? Being willing to consider forgiveness in the same breath as the offense is like a chink of light appearing in the armor of resentment allowing the flowers of forgiveness and rebirth to reach up toward the sun. It allows Grace to shine through. Sometimes this can only happen when we are exhausted, worn down far enough from holding the grudge.

Forgiveness involves looking at the event in greater context. Robert Enright of Wisconsin University writes "Forgiveness is a willingness to abandon one's right to resentment, negative judgement and indifferent behaviour toward one who unjustly injured us, while fostering the undeserved qualities of compassion, generosity and even love toward him. This sums up how big an `ask` it is, to willingly surrender the need to be right…"

When we can acknowledge that all judgment is really a judgment of self no matter how expertly we project it; and thus, all forgiveness is forgiveness of our shadow self, then the winner from choosing to forgive can only be us. This concept is huge. Once we are able to `own` our responses and our judgments, the stage is set for release of the pain.
In childhood, most of us were given many warnings and much advice; from studying hard to get a good job to earn a decent salary, to excessive alcohol consumption causing pain, and unprotected sex leading to diseases and/or pregnancy, or smoking being bad for our health. How many did we have to explore for ourselves f before we `got it`? If only we could learn from other's mistakes, humanity would be perfect! When we are able to start owning our actions, we may move toward taking responsibility for them and also, responsibility for releasing what no longer serves.

Forgiveness is complete when we can look upon the object of our projection, recall the past and happily embrace them. Time has been truncated, alchemical transformation has changed the memories of the past allowing freedom and movement. We have separated the sinner from the sin as Christianity urges us.

Father Jim McManus offers that we `accept through repentance the forgiveness which was there all along`. Repentance is a genuine sadness over previous actions. We have grown and recognized that our actions or words have been, in the Buddhist vernacular, less than skillful and we wish to make amends. Repentance is a catalyst for forgiveness.

Forgiving another is dependent on our willingness to see beyond their actions and our responses to the souls in pain beneath. Here is where the invisible comes to life through the expression and manifestation of Grace.

We can only forgive another as much as we are open to forgiveness for ourselves. The Lord's Prayer states this as the verb in the prayer, "Forgive us our trespasses AS we forgive others."

Forgiveness, often does not affect the other, but is a gracious healing liberation for the pain of the sufferer. It allows compassion to flow and heals the mind. As history is rewritten by the victors, so it is with our history. Is the ability to forgive the lens for our memoirs, perhaps a barometer of the spiritual journey?

Understanding the past or the wound does not change the future, or the present. Through Grace we can surrender and when we have surrendered ego control, we can forgive. This is a powerful combination, Grace, Surrender and Forgiveness.

Living fully in the now requires a healthy release of the past to offer us the freedom to be fully present to this very moment where time collapses and all is one. Caroline Myss summed this up when she said *"Without forgiveness you remain anchored in the past, forever in emotional debt."* Once we have stepped into forgiveness we experience true deep healing at the soul level.

We can do this by offering up a simple prayer. "Beloved God, Divine One, help me to want to forgive. Amen." The willingness to forgive is your soul speaking directly to the Divine despite the roaring cries of injustice, unfairness and self pity from the ego.

We are asking for help in forgiving, not asking God to do it for us. God has no need to forgive as there is nothing to forgive, but as humans we live in a dual world where many ego based reactions rule. Our ability to forgive is in equal balance with our ability to receive the forgiveness of God as we move towards a place of unity where forgiveness has no need to exist. We are trapped by our ego and how it dictates our self-worth. The spiritual journey guides us out of this predicament with each stage building towards the next as self-worth expands, forgiveness becomes easier and deeper, finally becoming obsolete as we move into complete integrity and union.

The Course in Miracles offers us a way to forgive, "Instead of trying to change myself or others, try forgiveness, forgiving myself and forgiving others. And if I can't forgive somebody (if my ego won't let me), then ask the Holy Spirit in me to forgive. It's like asking my higher Self to forgive others, and forgive me." The course concludes "God is the love in which I forgive" and "Fear binds the world, forgiveness sets us free".

Grace
Grace is an invisible, ethereal, sometimes undeserved, unasked for blessing from God. Grace is the Holy Spirit in action, silently transforming our lives. Grace moves us to behave in ways that enhance our soul, to forgive, to see beyond the chaos of the external world to a sacred life which is rich in meaning and purpose, and to have the courage to take action in the face of our doubt. The more open we are to divine flow, the more grace may move through us for the benefit of all.
Grace arises through divine connection and assists us when we struggle with stepping into our Highest place. Praying with humility, acknowledging that you cannot do it alone, may open

a portal to Grace. prayer is a conversation with God, Grace is God's reply. Grace transforms the inner world so that we see the sacred in everything. Grace is gentle and soft. Its impetus is always for healing, for enhancing your inner strengths.

Confession

Confession allows a person the chance to keep up to date with his own behavior, to employ his self-awareness to reflect on the past day, week or month, looking at where he could and wants to do better.

For some, confession is seen as a `get out of jail card`. Like all things, the value of an action depends on the intention behind it. Practices like confession have the potential to deepen over the years as we mature. Over time, confessing different thoughts, words or actions (as our expanded self-awareness allows us more access into our patterns) leads us deeper into the spiritual journey. Even the same action, may come from completely different motivations and beliefs, and over time may lead to deeper realizations.

Ill health comes where we step out of integrity and act on the ego, which often brings out shame in us. Without the benefit of friends and counselors to offer unconditional listening, witnessing our truth as we release the shame of our actions, we may hold on and store our `secrets`, which harden over the years and metastasize into illnesses.

Sharing with another about where we have slipped up may result in emotions which are very telling. It could be said that confession is to lance an emotional boil.

"*In the beginning was the word*", so starts the gospel of John in the New Testament. In all religious traditions there is an awareness of the power of vibration, from the "OM" of Buddhism to the "AUMM "of Hinduism. Science concurs that all the universe is vibration.

We use sound in word form as a way to connect with others. In confessing, the vibration of the speech is a release. The words, once spoken can never be taken back and a truth has been born.

No matter how right the truth is, once uttered, or even thought, it is there in the energetic soup of the cosmos forever.

Once a secret has been aired, it is no longer a secret. It's owner is free because he or she is no longer alone in the secret. Bound together, the confessor and confessee have offered and received honesty and unconditional acceptance, which together mitigate the power of the secret freeing the confessee from the past to an expanded future.

Discernment
What is my inner truth? How do I know? How can I follow the right path when there are so many tempting distractions? The ego knows you as well as you do and may produce very well justified explanations for doing what it wants.

Understanding the ego is important as we know how it limits us. Choices we make today dictate our tomorrows, their basis is crucial to our growth.

It is difficult to see fears directing our choices and yet be too immersed in the fear to make a different choice. Perhaps this would be a good time to pray for `willingness`?

It is so easy to believe that what we want is God's Divine Will for us. St John of the Cross says, "When confronted with a decision, take the path you like the least as therein lies most growth." I recall my dislike for this idea when I first encountered it! On further reflection, I have come to understand that a choice made in consideration of the long term greater good for all versus the short term good for myself brings greater peace and fulfillment.

Each thought, and therefore each discernment, comes from either love or a form of fear.

Experiential healing

True healing is experiential and holistic. If the human being is regarded as only a body and addressing the imbalance on the purely physical level is attempted, as many medications and diets do, failure often results in the long term.

As a species we run from pain. We seek to palliate and soothe, deny, suppress and distract, do whatever we can to avoid the pain and fear surrounding the portal to freedom and peace, honest self-awareness. This may be existence, but it isn't growth.

When life is not exactly as we want it to be, then it hurts. In reality, it is when life is not what the _ego_ wants (which is to be special), that the suffering begins.

Remember the heartbreak of the first love that didn't work out, our expectations became disappointments. Do we suppress the feelings, build a little wall around us and distract into new relationships? Can we invest 100% again or is it far too risky? Or do we feel the pain of loss and sadness of shattered dreams and allow our hearts to open and allow compassion to flow out, growing through the wounds of vulnerability?

Like riding a wave, moving from `I am sad` to `I feel sad` neither denies the pain through suppression, nor becomes the pain through over-identification with it.

When we enter into the experience of life, we can grow through it. In homoeopathic terms we see this engagement with the totality of life in the aggravation after a remedy. The remedy magnifies the expression of all the symptoms pushing the ego to the edge of its control, and only then can it fail, allowing us to get our ego out of the way of our growth. We grow through adversity. If we live in perfect worlds with perfect partners and perfect friends, we aren't really living at all. It is more of a `Stepford Wives` existence, remaining on the surface of life perpetually externalizing the search for acceptance and validation to the detriment of inner peace and soul connection.

Medicinal systems that take away the pain alone are suppressive, not only of the symptom itself, but of the soul, as our deepest expression of wholeness. Treating the physical symptoms as the only mode of expression being used by the Vital Force ignores our relationship with Soul and the Divine. It renders us pawns in a celestial game between two players, ego and God, when the truth is that we are extensions of the Divine being blinded by our own Free Will as experienced through the ego.

It's possible that when we choose to make a positive transformation in our lives, the inner saboteur will try to seduce us back to old ways. The function of the Mystic-Healer is to help us recognize the antics of the ego.

Families / relationships
Families and friends are a crucible for transformation at the soul level. Family are those with whom we have long term connections and a deep commitment to continuing relationship. It is very easy to distract ourselves from the vulnerability of people knowing us deeply by presenting a`new` version of ourselves that we accept and want others to see. When people might be getting too close or we cannot sustain the image of self we want to believe, either the ego crumbles and we open up into greater honesty, or we dive into another distraction to deflect others from seeing too deeply, or we become ill. In these ways, we prevent ourselves from accepting the gift that long term relationship offers.

Being seen is a double edged sword, all humans want to be seen, but it is also the greatest fear, opening us to potential rejection.

Here in the chalice of these relationships, we are safe to be fully human with all our warts. They have already seen us and not rejected us. This is the most similar experience on earth to the love God has for us.

Family is safety, loving us into an expansion of ourselves like a snake protected in hiding as it sheds its skin.
Because those closest to us know which buttons to press to get a rise out of us like nothing else, long term relationships that we choose to stay in are rich in opportunities for growth.

The quality of these relationships depends on the honesty of the people involved, as well as the depth of acceptance and knowingness combined to offer the most unconditional love we are capable of giving and receiving. It is here that the soul can grow, nourished by relationship, with opportunities for forgiveness, and the chances to give and receive unconditional love.

Soul growth is not about understanding, working it out and making it better, rather it is the transformation from who we think we are to whom we really are and our long term relationships are the catalyst for this change. Those closest to us reflect back an area of denial. We choose whether to embrace this reflection, or to stagnate and fester suffering from resistance to releasing the need to be right.

Yet at the end of the day, each person, be they family, friend, acquaintance or passer-by, is a facet of the Divine and the relationship we have with one, is the relationship we have with all. How we love the Divine in our lives is how we love everyone.

Mirroring

"You cannot know God the way you know anything else; you only know God or the soul of anything subject to subject, center to center, by a process of "mirroring" where like knows like and love knows love—"deep calling unto deep" (Psalm 42:7)." Father Richard Rohr writes and is reflecting the homoeopathic principle of `like cures like` at its deepest place.

The Sufis have a beautiful chant
> *"Let my heart reflect thy light Lord*
> *As the moon reflects the light of the sun in love"*

They believe that we are mirrors not only to each other, but also with the divine. Thus our only requirement as human beings is to polish our hearts so we can accurately reflect God's love, extending it out into the world.

If it is possible to project what we don't like out onto others; the reverse is also possible by focusing on where we see the good in others. This then transforms our tarnished self into gleaming glass offering a perfect reflection.

> ***If God is home, then the purpose of our sessions as***
> ***Mystical-Healers is tomirror home to the other,***
> ***to help them find themselves.***

Gifts of Health
Sacred awe

Life is truly magical. In nature, we have ample opportunities to observe this: the dewdrops on a rose at dawn, the sun setting over hills or water, clouds tinged pink and glowing in the liminal sky, the diamonds of snowflakes sparkling in a hard frost, or a shimmering rainbow. Children have a joy in living as they constantly see the wonder in a new sight, sound, smell etc.They lose themselves as separate and just become one in their sacred awe.

Beauty is a portal to the Divine, heaven lurks there and is all around us, it is just that we have forgotten to stop to notice the wonder we live in. Be it in a weed that has grown through a crack in a pavement to a fern sparkling with spray in a waterfall. All are equally awe-inspiring, however it is easier to notice the larger moments like the waterfall or a sunrise. The Sacred world is all around us. It is also within us and once we start to look within we see it in others. Life and health improve when you make the choice to see the sacred at all times; in the rainbows, in the bubbles when washing dishes, enjoying the glowing embers of wood you have sawn, fetched and chopped yourself, in seeing a child look their best in clothes you have washed and ironed. All seemingly mundane activities, yet when viewed through a different lens, they take on new meaning. The sacred is here all the time, it is mysterious and magical and it is up to us whether or not we see it. It is as simple as choosing to stop for a nanosecond and give the moment full attention.

Imagine a life where the ordinary becomes extraordinary. That is the world awaiting and all you have to do is choose.. choose and feel deep gratitude for the wonders you behold.

Freedom
Interdependence is our true place in the universe. As we get healthier, we consciously choose to live in closer alignment. We start to reverse society's mores and to become more authentically our true selves. We start to move towards freedom as we begin to re-value freedom and honour our own souls. We become more about who we are than what we do. We could do anything but *everything* we do is determined by our motivation and that defines how we do it.

Einstein says "Find your passion, make it your profession and you will never work again".

That is the very definition of freedom: living in your passion at all times. This is a life that is blessed. When we do what we love, life is flowing harmony. We spend so many hours a day at work that this is one of the most important decisions we ever make. We can all do many things. I could work in a bank, but the stress of it would cost me a small fortune in Gin!

The Divine has a plan for each of us and our integrity is related to our living fully within the plan. This does not mean that if we are not in the `perfect` job we are out of alignment, as alignment is much more about the quality of what we do than the details of what it is that we do. If we do whatever job we have with love, kindness, compassion and humor then the job is perfect. All of life, every situation, every job, every event is an opportunity to meet with ourselves and another.

The work we chose should be an extension of our true self, not from pressure by a Career Guidance person or a parent.

Many people have a sense they have been called to do something special in their lives. Yet when we look beneath the myriad people claiming celebrity status to the ones whose names are remembered and spoken of in years to come, they were and are the people who fully inhabit their Divine alignment. Nelson Mandela stuck to his beliefs, refused to be swayed and endured 27 years in a prison, such was his integrity. Had he recanted when arrested or in court would we know his name now? Consider the courage of Malala Yousafzai who stood up for education for women at a tender age. Her unshakeable dignity and integrity have propelled her into being known. Both are famed for who they are as much as what they did, their actions being manifestations of the depth of their integrity.

It is better to inner validate with your Divine calling and be known for integrity and willingness to stand up for your beliefs, than to court the media and live or die by their words. Nelson Mandela's book is titled `The Long Road to Freedom`, yet in truth he was free throughout his incarceration as his mind was always his own. This is true of Stephen Hawking, whose body imprisons him, while his mind is free to roam the universe. So many people are imprisoned by their own fears, regrets, resentments, and delusions. Their need for external validation chains them to the opinions of others.

Inter-dependence
The aim of life is inter-dependence, where giving and receiving are equal. Scientists call this state quantum entanglement, where no particles can be apart from other particles. Every atom in the universe is perpetually in sync with all other atoms. Nothing happens in isolation. Science has caught up with the mystics who have always known that we are all part of the One of humanity, and in fact, the universe.
If science now proves this, then what are the blocks preventing us from leading lives of deep trust? A life lived in deep trust would remove all the stress and pain of misplaced control.
But there is always that damn ego.

We are so blessed. Each day the sun rises anew and we can begin again, we can make the choice each day to do it differently. Each day we can discern our calling. Each day we can seek to embody it a little more deeply. We can make the conscious choice and ask for Divine guidance, offering a prayer of willingness to go deeper, just a little deeper each day.

Peace
Peace is heaven on earth. Peace is not something to achieve out there in another country, another town, another family or another person. It is to be surrendered to, in our hearts and minds, in our relationships and homes; it is in our thoughts and words, in our breathing and in the beating of our hearts.

The concept of peace is a yardstick of health. How at peace are you? Using that question as a model for continual reflection is a commitment to inner healing. Asking the question indicates a willingness to move deeper into peace, to highlight and release all that stands between you and peace, to allow everything to be just what it is. That doesn't mean we sit passively sucking our thumbs as the world goes to hell in a handbasket. It means we are able to apply the Serenity Prayer effectively.

"God, grant me the serenity to accept the things I cannot change,
Courage to change the things I can,
And wisdom to know the difference".

It is such a short prayer, yet so deeply powerful in releasing us from the unnecessary, the external and the ego. It hands over discernment to God removing one block on the road to peace.

Peace can be found on every level.
Physically, peace is being at one with your body. Does your body fit you like a slipper, comfortable and flexible or are you at war with it?

Mentally, peace is being unified in your thinking. Are you still wrapped up in the conditioning of childhood? It can be surprising how many familial `conditions` you might have still directing your life.

Emotionally, peace is being fully honest and in complete integrity in all you say and do. Are you dishonest in any way with yourself or others?

Before we can extend peace to the world, we need to find it within, to`be` peace in the world. We become the very presence of peace and need `do` nothing as our presence *IS* peace and speaks for us.

When we achieve personal peace it manifests in all of life, familial, societal, occupational, recreational, etc. We all continually impact each other. When we have chosen to find inner peace, we call others to meet us there. To change the world we must first change ourselves.

"Yesterday I was clever, so I wanted to change the world.
Today I am wise, so I am changing myself." Rumi

Humility

In the dictionary, humility is defined as the state of recognizing your own value and other's value equally. The word humility comes from the word humus, the earth itself. Humility is knowing that God lives in and through us. Everything has come from God, so the ego cannot take either the praise or blame.

False humility is the state of thinking we are less than other people. In the UK, false humility is encouraged as we are taught from children not to `get out of our place in life. Whilst the intention behind this was undeniably egalitarian, it has also encouraged society to suppress people from being true to their own passion. Humility and pride are opposites, yet pride can appear as humility when the ego plays small, as in false humility. Charles Dicken's character Uriah Heap and his obsequiousness is the perfect literary representation of this.

Mary, the mother of Jesus, is the most perfect example of pure humility. She trusts in God and accepts her mission with grace despite the social implications. Humility is releasing the ego and accepting that you are a divine child, good enough exactly as you are. In humility, there is remembrance that all comes from the Divine, whether good or bad. The Muslims have an expression they will say after every achievement, honour or complement, `Inshallah`, which means `if Allah wills it`. Not only is it to remember that all comes from God, it also stimulates an attitude of gratitude and helps prevent pride.

Therapeutic relationships

The Therapeutic-relationship is a role of receiving, of "being present to", of personal opening.

The relationship between practitioner and patient only becomes therapeutic when the invisible dynamic of compassion is activated. Once compassion is involved then the relationship becomes therapeutic for *both* parties.
Physician, heal thyself is so much more than applying a plaster to a cut. It refers to healing at the deepest level, that of the soul.

The therapeutic relationship is not just confined to practice. Every interaction between two people no matter what the situation, has the potential to be a healing encounter. Therapeutic relationships happen when practitioners are fully committed to their own healing.

Responsibility

Healers, due in part to their caring natures, tend to take on responsibility that is not theirs, to become overly responsible for the healing outcome of the other. As healers, we may find ourselves in a place of 'ego caring' where our ego is uncomfortable seeing another in pain, or we may find ourselves in a place of 'ego power' where there is attachment to being seen as being successful at helping.

It is hard to remain detached enough to allow another their own healing crisis in whatever form it takes and just offer a silent holding space. This is what genuine compassion offers. In previous chapters, we have touched on the ways the ego insidiously derails us. For example, how do we reconcile caring about our patients and being detached enough not to take responsibility for their healing process?

Response-ability is the ability to respond to appropriately others. When we cannot release the other, the expectations our responsibility imposes become the energetic limitation on the potential of their freedom.

One group I worked with years ago came up with a definition of the perfect homoeopath, *"The perfect homoeopath loves unconditionally and doesn't care what happens"*. They do their very best and then release any expectation of outcome and allow the Vital Force to do whatever it needs to do which, of course, it knows and we do not.

It is very important to explore the role of responsibility in the therapeutic relationship as many practitioners reach burn out when they remain overly responsible. No-one can hold the life of another in their hands, let alone maybe hundreds of people without burning out.

One way to determine if you are taking too much responsibility is to ask how you feel after seeing a patient, do you feel tired or invigorated? Tiredness indicates that on some level some of what you are doing is coming *from* you. Feeling invigorated indicates that the Divine has been flowing *through* you allowing a mutuality of healing.

Responsibility begins and ends with us, we are responsible for our bodies, minds and hearts in physical health, fitness, understanding and emotions. As previously stated, each thought we have leads us either closer to fear or closer to love, our only responsibility is to make the choice for love. This choice is being made in every second of every minute.

I saw a friend brimming over with happiness, who told me in utter delight that she had made the decision for God. We met for coffee a couple of days later and she was deeply saddened. She had really thought that saying yes to God was all she had to do, she hadn't realized she would have to keep saying yes again and again. The relationship with God is made up of billions of yeses, constantly choosing love over fear in each thought, word and decision.

Presence

The world of the soul is empathic, connective and flowing. The soul holds the vision for life. In a state of health, our minds are servants to the vision of our soul.

It is reported that only 10% of communication is verbal. 90% of communication comes through body language, facial inflections and the `energetic aura` each emits. This might be as obvious as the degree of someone's engagement with us, or it could be as subtle as the unconscious `knowingness` of how much we can reveal through words to another before being judged.

The Tao says being fully here is the Zen of living. In the therapeutic relationship, we chose to consciously be fully present to the other, releasing our own thoughts and concerns to give full attention to the other. Only when we are present mentally, physically and emotionally are we `whole`. From this wholeness, we can be fully present, awake on all levels allowing us to be a presence.

Holding presence demonstrates unconditional love and deep respect. If our defenses are down, it allows the other to meet us there. If we embrace acceptance, the other will feel seen, heard and held, and in that moment, the healing begins.

When our soul emerges in our broken places, the ones we usually hide the most, and we are with someone who is fully present to us, healing happens naturally. Steeping the deepest pain in the energy of the deepest love is the heart of healing - therapeutic relationship at its highest.

Fully present here and now, everything is perfect. In the now, there are no fears nor worries nor pain, as the past and future do not exist. Behold the reflection of compassionate love in the eyes of the other, this is the gift of now, the eternal moment that lasts forever.

The whole comprises the soul, intellect and body. The body is the affirming force. It engages with the world through inhaling air, by eating and drinking, through touch and making love, all of which are to open to give and receive with the other.

The heart is not only for personal expression, it is also for divine perception. An opened whole heart is a dynamic healing tool, it is being a presence for God.

The Dance of Healing
A dance of healing is a poetic visual description of what is going on in the therapeutic relationship. The relationship is a mutuality that creates its own impetus, a dynamic shared by both parties that will last until they have `healed` each other, however long that may be.

Our very existence is a dance. Between birth, when we separate from our mother, and the time we find a soul mate, we move closer and back away in many relationships. A soul mate will dance the dance of duality with us aiming for transforming it into the dance of full immersion, `someone` to come home to, to be a part of.

The unconscious dynamic of life is to heal the separation we have from God. The therapeutic relationship heals this separation when the recognition is made that the other is also us. Together there is the ebb and flow, each `truth` they surrender to us in trust requires our equal surrender in acceptance. In this dance, we invite the Divine to teach us the steps. Our mutual surrender is held in the trust we offer, in highlighting for each other a block to receiving and therefore giving pure love. Giving and receiving are one, we can only give to the same degree that we can receive.

Within each relationship is the power to change the world. Offering and receiving healing transforms duality into one perfect entity that dances in perfect rhythm, so close they are as one.

With each circuit of the dance floor, we learn the steps and the other's rhythm more intimately. Each visit we learn additional subtlety of language, the nuance of their honesty, we go with them, then we pull them back, we highlight and release in a flowing continual movement always deepening until finally reaching the core truth of who they are. And we hold them in perfect harmony and safety as we are held.

In physical crisis the body produces adrenaline
In mental crisis there is burn out
In emotional crisis there is hysteria
In spiritual crisis...the dark night of the soul
Death and rebirth – cellular, day and night etc... dance of
duality
Power of choice and the essence of the mystical cycle of death
and rebirth

Speaking and listening
We live in a world full of words, often with little of substance being said and no-one listening.
Speaking and listening are also a dance, a dance of vibration and energy. The speaker leads and the listener follows.
Speaking and listening reflect the yin and yang of life itself.
Speaking is active dynamic and projected, while listening is receiving, it is gentle and still.

It can be said that speech is vibration, represents the masculine energy, is an emanation of YOU, you `in-action`. If speech is "I" then listening becomes feminine, it is YOU, you `in-receiving`.

The words we utter may or may not be in alignment with our soul, if they aren't, they are ego based. Words are one vehicle the ego uses to project fears outwards. We can use words as swords and cut like a knife, or as gentle loving balm to the soul. If we physically speak a lie, the words create a vibration that not only extends out on the very breath of the word, but also reverberates within us. When our words come from love, the outward flow of energy is harmonious with no separation

between us and our soul, diffusing the physical boundaries between us and the entire universe. When we lie or speak words in contradiction to our soul, the reverberation of the lie reinforces a barrier between us and the outside world.
Listening is a gift we can offer to ourselves and to others. The experience of being listened to validates our existence. When we listen, we offer a dynamic healing tool – the presence of `I am here; I hear you`. Feeling heard and feeling held makes us feel alive.

Beyond helping others, beyond offering respect, when we fully listen to another, *we are listening to ourselves*. The other is always a reflection of our own interior, every word spoken is also our word.

Truly listening requires more than not speaking, it is a dynamic state of complete emptiness where we have released preconceived notions, ideas, and judgments. If we are listening, we are not formulating what we will say next in the conversation. There is no desire to better the other in wit, experience, or cleverness nor an intention to put another down. The ego has no place in true listening.

Listening is deep, deep allowing, not just of the words which arise, but allowing the other to recount what they need to, as deeply as they need to, and at their own pace. We do not encourage or discourage, we accept and allow. In stillness we cannot lend judgment or opinion, we cannot say things that cannot be retracted. The silence necessary for this deep therapeutic listening requires humility, releasing any ego involvement leaves us humble, open to deep revelation from the other.

Confuscious says that silence is oxygen for the soul. A powerful image indeed, without silence we can neither hear the small still voice of God, nor the wounded heart of a friend.
Stillness is the bedrock from which soul listening emerges to the benefit of all.

The most needed skills of Therapeutic relationship practitioners are knowing what to ask and being able to listen. Using the fewest questions necessary to elicit the person's disconnection from soul, and the ability to fully hear and be present to the response, are essential in practice and also in personal and spiritual growth.

" it is far more valuable to speak to God than to speak about God for there is much self love in spiritual conversations "
Teresa of Lisieux

Trust and surrender
In the therapeutic relationship there are two words that arise constantly: surrender and trust. Our role is to be so utterly trustworthy that the other instinctively senses that they can trust us with their truth. Surrendering ego ensures we hear the truth as it is spoken. Any word in excess of what is required is a boulder in the flow of trust. Every distracted look or gesture adds to the detritus in the river of communication. Without ego, we are more able to maintain holistic awareness of the other and a greater degree of presencing with them. We are fully present to witness, receive and reflect in this holiest of places, the therapeutic relationship. The honour this bestows on the other is the ability to dive deeper, the honour this bestows on us is the ability to receive the deepest, most honest case affording us a greater chance to find the true similimum.

If healing is discovering our true self, our role as Mystic-Healers is to create an environment conducive to self-awareness by surrendering any preconceived idea of how the session might go, what clever thing we can say, what insights we can offer; in short, our role is to release ego disguised as expectation.

It takes practice and courage to surrender and sit in the mystery of not knowing what the person will say and have faith that what they say is also our story. We create sacred space, we listen with the ears of the heart. We listen to their stories. We go with their flow as they purge the past through speech. We merge their wounds with ours feeling the pain together and then, holding hands, we release the pain. We surrender the wound to the past, a past we have blessed with forgiveness and now our bodies can release the memories.

Doing anything less is trifling with the other, moving symptoms around without genuine healing effected. It is never what I do for you, it is always what we do for us. We are not separate, we are facets of the Divine meeting and coming together, think of the power emitted when two particles come together in the Hadron Collider. Now scale it up to human size! That is potential far beyond our conceptual thinking.

Healing is a homecoming. The therapeutic relationship, through shared experience, propels this forward for both people. Together anything is possible.

When ego meets ego, it may appear a shared experience, but each is experiencing it alone. Ego meeting ego produces a magnetic repulsion, a stand off. In pain, it is a magnetic attraction. In our wounds we draw the other to us and feel their wounds. We step out of false illusion, and meet them where they are in this moment, this very present `now`. There is nothing else but the two of us in naked egoless union. What healing there is in humility when we can see beyond the body to the innocent soul, the indwelling Divine.

Willingness alone indicates the knowledge that there must be a better way thus opening the door to the inner world where healing takes place. Willingness starts the conversation. When all is going well, we rarely question our delusion that we are in control and God is made in our image. It is when things fail that the cracks in life show. This could happen through a job loss, a divorce or an emotional trauma or crisis.

Mastery of the Arts

Holy inquiry is the goal of case taking. It is easy to bombard our patient with questions, grill them lightly and fry their brains, yet what do we achieve? Nothing but what they want us to know which, if they become overwhelmed; will be nothing more than self-preservation.

Ideally we want them to share their sense of inner disconnect from their soul and that requires a different approach. To ask to be invited in is to respect their privacy and also to acknowledge that it is in the deep places that the healing occurs. We knock upon their heart and ask for entry, the more humble and respectful we are, not just in asking, but in our souls, the wider the door is opened as our heart is allowed entry to merge in defenselessness.

The Mystic-Healer is committed to mastering the art of inquiry and mastering the art of really listening, seeing, touching, and feeling. One knows that the case lies in the questions asked. The questions are keys to unlock the defenses revealing the deeper self.

When we listen to the others soul and ask the questions we ask, we are also asking and listening for the answer within ourselves. The other, in their story, has provided a reflection of ourselves that previously we were unable to see.

It is very important that the Mystic-Healer knows where she is going in her own journey. It gives a framework for the questions she will ask. It is well worth spending time in gaining clarity in this and creating some questions that will focus the case to elicit what you need to know, remembering that the person is often not with us for the reason they think they are.

Our authenticity determines the depth of their vulnerability; *our* secrets limit their freedom of speech. I am aware that this has been touched on previously, however it is such a vital component of being a Mystic-Healer that it bears repetition.

Every lie we tell ourselves suppresses the Divine flow and weakens our connection. Christ was 100% Divine *because* he was 100% human, he was able to be fully in the moment and angry when angry. It wasn't his perfection that made him divine, it was his fully owned imperfections that made him divine.

Again it is, 'physician know thyself'.

This depth of interaction will bring to the surface all manner of suppressed shames and secrets for which a person may seek some level of absolution from the practitioner, conscious or unconscious, as the practitioner is the one to have heard them. As the client is reflecting back to the practitioner, it may well happen that they verbalize some of the practitioner's secrets and shames that only come to consciousness as they are spoken and heard. Hence the need for personal supervision, spiritual direction or a regular place to work through these uprisings is vital to the quality of the practitioner's wellbeing and practice. Hearing the other with a willingness to own that this is also our struggle opens the healing potential. The Twelve Step Programme addresses this very issue, of soul searching, honesty, reparation, and atonement deeply and effectively. Father Richard Rohr has written a powerful book entitled "Breathing under Water" which is well worth a read.

The Mystic-Healer

"Mysticism, in its purest form, is a science of ultimates, the science of union with the Absolute, and nothing else, and that the mystic is the person who attains to this union, not the person who talks about it. Not to know about, but to Be, is the mark of the real initiate" Evelyn Underhill

"Mysticism is a revelation of the eternal in the midst of the temporal"
Brother Wayne Teasdale

The Mystic-Healer plays many roles beyond those discussed in the Therapeutic relationship. In addition to the receptive, allowing model, the Mystic-Healer offers a more dynamic role as one willing to confront, to invite accountability, to offer guidance, to create ritual and ceremony and to teach through example.

Mystic-` ministry` is healing as it opens to the suffering, the loneliness and pain meeting the other there. It reminds us of our brokenness, where our potential healing lies, the door to liberation. It is a hard place to be present to because the instinctual urge is to protect another from pain, not hold their hands and jump in with them. Yet this is pure homoeopathy, `Like cures Like` propelling towards an aggravation to which the only way out is through ego surrender allowing the Divine to flow inwards. The Mystic-Healer, in a deep desire for union with all, joins with the other at their deepest place and together their souls merge.

Mysticism

Mysticism is the practice of being `home,`
home with God.

The essence of mysticism is that the deepest part of your being is a part of the universal Oneness. Mystics are aware that we are

116

as timeless as God. Mysticism is the direct and actual experience of union. It is a dissolving of the ego, leaving the soul in perfect integrative harmony with itself and other. This union of conscious and unconscious, will and emotion, intellect and body transforms all to love and compassion, mercy and kindness.

Mystics believe that we are each a piece of the hologram of God, the microcosm of the macrocosm. Mysticism transcends the limits of rational thought. It could be said that fact is one-dimensional, while mystery is multi-dimensional, utterly limitless.

For many years a separation between the worlds of mysticism and science has existed. It is only recently through the discovery of quantum physics that science is proving the inter-connectedness of all atoms and particles down to thoughts being the conductor of the universe, as evidenced in the `observer effect`where the outcome of an experiment is altered by the presence of an observer. While science does not yet `prove` God exists, current leading edge science does suggest there is universal inter-connectedness.

Henri Nouwen said "Mysticism and revolution are two aspects of the same attempt to bring about radical change. One aspect is at the personal level and one at the level of society." Add to this Gandhi's exhortation to `Be the change you want to see`, and it becomes clear that personal change precedes change in society.

The mystic sees life and death as part of the duality of life. Cells die and are renewed on a daily basis, just as the dawn rises, bringing forgiveness and fresh hope each day.
The mystic sees the rational, and also sees beyond the rational, resting comfortably in the mystery of not knowing. His perception of life is through the lens of peace, harmony, creativity, love and renewal. This worldview offers healing through release of the illusions that we can control the external world. With surrender as the portal to healing, the mystic has stepped consciously through.

The mystic's purpose is to know herself at the level of the soul and to then use this awareness in service to others. The symbiosis of life is in our giving and equally in our receiving. The mystic dives fully into the cosmic soup, and in so doing becomes calm in chaos, love in hatred, faithful in doubt, compassion in pain and hope in despair. He lives in personal integrity and is open to channel Grace. This is the forefront of his raison d'etre, he choses to live consciously with God in service.

Mysticism transcends any individual religion. It is the perennial philosophy that is at the core of every tradition, the meeting point for mystics. Non-dual mind is a modern way of referring to the paradox of embracing the whole yet still seeing the parts, mysticism in practice. In the Philokalia, a collection of spiritual writings from the Christian East, it is described as *"Putting the mind into the heart"* rather than separating mind and heart. Cynthia Bourgeault phrases it as understanding ` heart as spiritualised mind, the organ prepared by God for contemplation`.

Calling
Some jobs we just do. Other jobs we feel compelled towards. `Calling` comes from the Latin `Fungi` meaning to carry out, to execute.

For many of us involved in the world of healthcare, we are responding to a calling from an inner voice `calling` us home to which we have answered `YES`. Perhaps this is the only true element of free will we have, the free will to decide when we will return home to God.

Home is the healed place within where we are One with God. The calling is our invitation to represent the Divine on earth by living this paradigm.

When we have said yes to this calling, the universe brings us the people needed to help us see the shadow sides of ourselves that we have denied. Blessed with a reflection of the blocks to pure love, we may then choose to embrace and heal. It is nothing short of a miracle which we accept when deciding to enter into the world of health and healing and give away to each person we meet when we offer the reflection we are for them.

Every passion that is lived is a miracle, no matter what the external expression of the calling. There is healing inherent in the `how` of what is done. It is the quality of the doing that is the catalyst for healing. What matters is finding *your* unique path.

When we love what we do, it is easy to get up each day, to have a spring in our step and a smile on our faces. It is like living life in a pair of slippers, it just fits, it's comfy and flexible. We are in deep alignment, which means everything is achieved to the power of ten!

Being in the right job is an expression of our state of mind. Once our thinking is aligned to our Highest Self, our words and actions follow. Once we have identified our passion, and have chosen to honour it, we live the resonance of our passion in our speech and actions. It all starts and ends with passion.

Our role as a Mystic-Healer is to remind people of their divine mission and to help them return to it. Living out of alignment opens a space for sickness to manifest. The best way to address sickness is in the correction of the worldview, to refocus on how the inner Divine may shine through us.

Jesus, Buddha, Gandhi and Mandela grew to be the embodiment of their beliefs. Jesus became love, Buddha became enlightenment, Gandhi became peace and Mandela became forgiveness.
This also applies to negative thinking as, to give just one example, Hitler became fear. The road to heaven is heaven and

the road to hell is hell. It is common for people to hop and skip between the paths of heaven and hell, moving yet not getting very far.

Thoughts may be invisible yet they determine who we are and what we do. Our role, as the observer in the practice room, is to 'be' unconditional love, influencing how the person is able to be with us and also with themselves. The practice room is the laboratory for miracles. When love is manifest, it reveals ego-manifestation and doubt, leaving a space for transmutation to occur.

Nothing is done in a vacuum. *Every* thought lands somewhere and has an effect. It is a lot to take on board, that everything we think, let alone say or do, is affecting the universe. With free will comes the responsibility to choose our thoughts wisely.

Thomas Moore said that finding the 'right' work for yourself is finding your soul in the world.
Caroline Myss sums up a 'calling' in health care perfectly, "The seeker, though in search of healing knowledge, was unknowingly also knocking on the door of mystical transformation."

Humility
A mystic can be recognized by humility. Humility comes when we have stepped into a bigger picture of reality and can see creation as an expression of the Divine, releasing our attachments to man-made distractions and ego desires. Humility frees from the need to defend and to externally validate.

Teaching
In practice, the Mystic-Healer exemplifies their mysticism in the simple presence of their being-ness. This draws clients wanting to know the how and what of the Mystic-Healer's inner peace. Humankind is always searching, consciously or unconsciously, for that inner place of peace. Once it is seen, it will evoke many questions. A Mystic-Healer teaches in

response to questions. They do not preach or dictate, they live in Grace, teaching by example. Being in simple presence is offering a lived experiential understanding to another who can then take from it what they will.

As every word we speak comes from the depth of our belief, the Mystic-Healer cannot help but speak from the heart, revealing her humility, awe and wonder. The Mystic- Healer speaks beyond the intellectual need to know, to the mystery of trust in soul surrender. She takes us through mere meaning to the reflective subtle nuance the soul enjoys.
Soul to soul teaching is osmotic, fusion without confusion.

Wisdom
Wisdom is the realm of integration. Knowledge, it is said, is power, however knowledge and experience together are wisdom. When we are stuck in ego, we are static, wisdom offers the way out. In wisdom, we meet fame and failure equally, and understand that life is what it is and is always changing. There is no need for dependency on others to save it, nor independence from others. We are one and together in wisdom, anything is possible.

Tools for the Mystic -Healer
Mystic-Healers live a `Divine-centric`life, with the aim of `living in the world while not being of the world`. Because modern life pervasively challenges this mission, a framework to help us stay centered on the Divine is essential.

Religious and spiritual traditions recognize the need for time out. We all need time out to make sense of the chaos of the world, of our life, of our thinking. With so much external bombardment, the senses become tattered and it can be impossible to clearly hear the small still voice of God.
Time out allows for percolation of our experience into our hearts, transforming it into wisdom. Regular explorations of belief in accordance with conscious knowledge is a gift we offer ourselves and others.

The Power of Ritual.

Life, with no beginnings and endings, like a book with no commas or full stops, let alone paragraphs and chapters, begins to blur and run ramshackle into the nonsensical. It could be said that ritual is the grammar of life.

We employ ritual many times a day as we go about our activities. We have a rhythm to cleaning our teeth, dressing, or preparing our food or tea. We greet people, then seal the verbal interaction with a farewell. There is ritual in shopping as we inquire, then acknowledge assistance by use of appreciation. An energetic bubble is created that contains the interaction.

Imagine a conversation that begins with no greeting and has no ending, the energies created by two people merging and swirling their individual auras would spill over if we did not employ conscious and unconscious techniques, ensuring that we retain our energetic integrity. Without this, our energy would be as diffused as a 40 watt energy saving light bulb. When we ensure definition in our energetic boundaries, we are able to focus our energies powerfully. This transforms the meaningless into a powerful energetic exchange.

Ritual can transition us from intellect into the heart. It may bring consciousness to action if it is performed in a state of awareness. It is this ritual that completes the triad of thought, word and deed.

Everything that happens in the world affects us. When we are not susceptible, we move in equal and opposite measure, retaining pivotal balance. When something happens that `rings our bells`, we often mis-react either discharging too much inappropriate energy into the universe, or suppressing the same amount of inappropriate energy by stashing it in our cells. What does this have to do with ritual?

Ritual is talking to our soul. It offers a conscious decision to grow. Each time we are less than authentic we incur energetic costs. In order to remain healthy, we should first `know thyself` and then, ` to thine own self be true`. Ritual is one way of re-establishing balance, bringing us back to conscious authenticity.

Rituals are a vital aid in the transitions in and out of relationships, with people, places, and things.

Ritual can also be a vehicle for forgiveness. It is not necessary to have both parties of the situation present as the ritual is for the individual. We cannot expect another's forgiveness, that is theirs alone to confer. It might mitigate our guilt temporarily to be forgiven, but we wouldn't need their forgiveness if we hadn't judged ourselves guilty.

You may remember a time when you agonised at length about something you had done to another, building up towards confession and then have experienced complete deflation as they tell you they hadn't really noticed. Equally, there are situations when we have been blamed and felt totally confused as we had seen ourselves as completely innocent and working to the highest of intentions!

Forgiveness of another is forgiveness of self in disguise. The adversary need not be there, let alone willing to dispense absolution.

The Mystic-Healer will actively encourage another to create and use ritual as part of their healing process. The Mystic-Healer might offer to be part of that creative process in support of those less creative or whom are unsure of how to proceed.

Visionary

Most people need three things in life. They need to be seen clearly, and so validate their existence; to be truly heard; and to be held in unconditional love and acceptance. The Mystic-Healer holds the vision for the other by seeing the truth of who they are no matter how they present. He is able to see beyond the other's fears to the expanded world of their true potential. This vision offers a yardstick for the other's personal accountability.

This is a powerful role. Clients sometimes focus on physical symptoms and struggle to see beyond them. They come to us through an energetic process unconsciously knowing that the vision we hold will support them through their healing process. Our vision anchors us both in the mystical world of union, trust and surrender, able to rest in the mystery.

Reverence

Reverence is seeing the world through the eyes of the Divine, the eyes of love.
Every one of us reveres something. In the world of the therapeutic relationship, we are choosing to revere the Divine within each of us, awake at all times to the Sacred as seen in everyday things. This way of perceiving the world leads us from ordinariness to extra-ordinariness.

Prayer

Religious traditions have set prayers, a form of liturgy that creates a framework for living. Some prayers are more formulaic and can be said almost bypassing conscious awareness in rote recitation; some prayers are from the heart in the moment; others bookend the day; others are in gratitude or petitionary. Prayers involve time out to speak with your Higher Power in whatever form that takes.

Prayers have been proven to speed recovery in patients after surgery. In homeopathy, the potency of the remedy is similar to the power of prayer. Prayer activates the Holy Spirit as much as the remedy acts on the Vital Force. As the Vital

Force is the `human` end of the Holy Spirit, we could conclude that prayer is a remedy as much as a remedy is. A prayer may contain no material substance, yet it goes straight to the core of life itself. The intention behind the prayer activates it, just as succussion transforms gross material matter into the homeopathic remedy. Prayer goes to the energetic realm where all is truly One.

Prayer time is when we remember our place in the scheme of things. It is our daily surrender to the Divine, a place of humility. As the Divine responds to the slightest willingness, imagine the power possible when we have set the stage for each session with a client in prayer; "Beloved One, help me be fully present to this person, my heart open and willing to be as one that we may heal together and return home. Thank you Amen."

This creates a container for the session, transforming our practice room into sacred space, gifting both with healing intention held in Divine love, allowing miracles to happen. The willingness that prayer can offer is the opening the Holy Spirit needs to reach through the cacophony of the discordant day to unite with the soul.

Meditation
Prayer is often considered religious, meditation is more often associated with spirituality. In truth, they both live in both places. Prayer is speaking to God, meditation can be said to be listening for God's reply, reflecting the truth of us in the Divine and the Divine in us.
Meditation is spending time with God, as it focuses on stilling the mind, releasing attachment to thought, becoming silently aware of the internal chatter and choosing not to engage with the thoughts. No matter what we pray for, unless we find time in stillness, we will never hear the guidance that God is offering in response to our prayer.

In meditation we may recognize our thought patterns and be able to discern between those that come from ego and those that come from our soul. Meditation helps us choose our thinking, which allows us to choose our lives.

There is a meditation practice that is homoeopathic called Tonglen meditation. It originated in India and has been practiced in Tibet since the eleventh century. Tonglen is a Tibetan word that literally means "sending and taking." In Tonglen practice, when we see or feel suffering, we breathe it in with the notion of completely feeling it, accepting it, and owning it. Then we breathe out, radiating compassion, loving-kindness, freshness; anything that encourages relaxation and openness.

It is `like curing like` in the meeting of our own or another's pain and suffering, to merge with the pain and the other and release it. Through owning and experiencing the pain and suffering, it can be healed and released. In this way, Tonglen meditation offers itself as a remedy.

Contemplation
Contemplation is a form of conscious percolation. Reflecting on a word or a few lines, pausing to allow them to resonate through our minds, bringing to mind all the meanings, diving deeply into the words and the images they induce allows for a renewed interpretation, and a deeper integration.

Daily life has become more hectic, with the senses continually assaulted. It is increasingly difficult to focus on only one thing at a time. There was a time when men fished and women knitted offering them each times of contemplation; hands occupied, yet minds still to reflect and contemplate. Knitting and fishing are a form of meditation-in-motion offering transformation of action into wisdom and spiritual growth. Today's moving meditations might include flow yoga, tai chi, qi gong, dance or climbing. All are embodied ways to contemplate.

Healing modality

There is a saying that "The tool is no more the healing than the finger pointing at the moon is the moon." It is easy to lose sight of the spiritual world and start to believe that the material is the start and end of life and rely on physical tools, pills and potions to cure us. Intriguingly, the western world is focused on saving the body with little thought for the mind, let alone the soul. I wonder if the uprising in popularity of zombie films is related in any way to our experience of the world?

Even in homoeopathy, whilst we accept that the remedies are dynamic, potent and very powerful, we still believe that we need to take a physical pill to ensure it works. Yet how many times have we heard from our patients` of improvement prior to taking the remedy and congruent with the moment we decided what remedy to give? Was our thinking of the prescription a prayer for them? How powerful is unconditional loving intention?

We have been exploring the re-merging of health and healing with the spiritual journey, we see that while Medicine may `fix` the body, it is Belief that saves the soul.

I would suggest that whatever medicinal model we use, it is the `how` of what we do that is the healing dynamic.

The medicinal system itself is merely a vehicle through which to meet people; people who are sent by Divine intervention in order that we see ourselves. The healing comes as we learn to love ourselves exactly as we are.

Deepak Chopra sums this up beautifully when he says, *"The wonder and the privilege of being a practitioner is being present when the God of human being, and just as accurately, the human God of being shows up"*

The Mystic-Healer has chosen to step into conscious growth and full commitment to her spiritual journey in order to fully serve others. She has explored and experienced the healing dynamic of self awareness, honesty, integrity, compassion, forgiveness, grace, authenticity, simplicity, therapeutic ritual, reverence, presence-ing and humility for herself. Thus she is able to open up her energetic field to welcome and reach out to the other, to join together on the return journey home.

The Mystic-Healer is one who sees the Divine in everyone and meets them there.

Introducing the Way of the Mystic-Healer, a year long mentored journey for those who wish to step consciously into the role of the Mystic-Healer. It comprises individual sessions, group sessions, reading, study, and sacred activism. It's aim is to take you on an experiential journey into yourself.

For more details go to
www.themystichealer.co.uk

Thank you for reading
Judith Wills
judeanna@gmail.com

Recommended Reading

Tao of Healing	Haven Trevino
All Sickness is Homesickness	Dianne Connoly
Anatomy of Spirit	Caroline Myss
A Return to Love	Marianne Williamson
Seeds of Contemplation	Thomas Merton
I and Thou	Martin Buber
Grace and Grit	Ken Wilbur
A Course in Miracles	Foundation for Inner Peace

Lightning Source UK Ltd.
Milton Keynes UK
UKHW02f1352190818
327434UK00005B/384/P